Foucault & the Political

This is the first comprehensive review of Michel Foucault's political thought within a single volume. *Foucault and the Political* explores Foucault's politics and political theories across the whole range of his writings, including material only recently made available.

Foucault's impassioned critique of the limitations of contemporary society and his affirmation of new forms of subjectivity have made his work vital to many areas of new political thinking – thinking that often operates outside conventional political categories. Jon Simons places Foucault's work in the context of contemporary political theory – including that of Michael Walzer, Charles Taylor and Jürgen Habermas – and examines it in relation to the rise of alternative models for politics – such as those found in the work of William Connolly and Judith Butler.

The political ramifications of Foucault's thought and the question of his personal politics have recently shaken up the way in which his work is understood. According to Simons, Foucault's concern with limits as both constraining and enabling and with transgression as a both theoretical and personal project is evident throughout his life and work.

Foucault and the Political includes concise explanations of key Foucauldian concepts, such as power/knowledge, subjectification, aesthetics of existence and political rationality. It will appeal to both the student and the more advanced reader in philosophy and politics, be they interested in Foucault or in contemporary political thought.

Jon Simons teaches political philosophy and feminist theory at the Hebrew University of Jerusalem.

Thinking the Political

General editors:
Keith Ansell-Pearson, *University of Warwick*
Simon Critchley, *University of Essex*

Recent decades have seen the emergence of a distinct and challenging body of work by a number of Continental thinkers that has fundamentally altered the way in which philosophical questions are conceived and discussed. This work poses a major challenge to anyone wishing to define the essentially contestable concept of 'the political' and to think anew the political import and application of philosophy. How does recent thinking on time, history, language, humanity, alterity, desire, sexuality, gender and culture open up the possibility of thinking the political anew? What are the implications of such thinking for our understanding of and relation to the leading ideologies of the modern world, such as liberalism, socialism and Marxism? What are the political responsibilities of philosophy in the face of the new world (dis)order?

This new series is designed to present the work of the major Continental thinkers of our time, and the political debates their work has generated, to a wider audience in philosophy and in political, social and cultural theory. The aim is neither to dissolve the specificity of 'the philosophical' into 'the political' nor to evade the challenge that 'the political' poses the 'the philosophical'; rather, each volume in the series will try to show how it is only in the relation between the two that new possibilities of thought and politics can be activated.

Future volumes will examine the work of Gilles Deleuze, Jacques Derrida, Luce Irigaray, Julia Kristeva, Ernest Laclau and Chantal Mouffe, Emmanuel Levinas and others.

Foucault & the Political

Jon Simons

London and New York

First published 1995
by Routledge
11 New Fetter Lane, London EC4P 4EE

Simultaneously published in the USA and Canada
by Routledge
29 West 35th Street, New York, NY 10001

© 1995 Jon Simons

Typeset in Sabon by
Florencetype Ltd, Stoodleigh, Devon

Printed and bound in Great Britain by
T J Press Ltd, Padstow, Cornwall

British Library Cataloguing in Publication Data
A catalogue record for this book is available from the British Library.

Library of Congress Cataloging in Publication Data
A catalogue record for this book has been requested.

ISBN 0–415–10065–8 (hbk)
ISBN 0–415–10066–6 (pbk)

Contents

Acknowledgements

This book is the fruition of much previous work and of all the support I received along the way. Yaron Ezrahi advised me through a Master's thesis and a doctoral dissertation on Foucault, employing a technique of 'constructive confusion' in order to foster my intellectual independence – from Foucault as well as himself. Without his patience and encouragement, this book would not have been written. The Israeli Political Science Association encouraged me to develop my work on Foucault by awarding me a prize for my Master's thesis in 1989. I was able to devote most of my time to my dissertation during 1990–2 thanks to a scholarship from the Planning and Grants Committee of the Israel Council for Higher Education. I was once again encouraged morally and financially to develop my research into a book when my dissertation was awarded the Bloomfield prize by the Hebrew University. The manuscript of this book was finally written while I enjoyed the financial support of Fulbright and Lady Davis postdoctoral fellowships, as well as the hospitality of the Government Department at Harvard.

The final version of the book has benefited from the helpful remarks of my dissertation readers – Aryeh Botwinick, Fred Dallmayr and Yaron Ezrahi – and of the editors of the series in which this book appears. The section on Foucault and feminism in Chapter 9 benefited from the comments of the participants of Bonnie Honig's graduate seminar in contemporary feminist theory at Harvard during 1992–3. My position on Foucault's conceptualization of resistance was clarified through conversations with Cynthia Chataway and Paul Routledge, both associated with Harvard's Program on Nonviolent Sanctions during the same year. Finally, I would like to thank Naomi Friedman for making her editorial skills available at the stage when the manuscript was too long and time too short.

A Note About Citations in the Text

Works by Foucault are cited in the text as dates only, and are listed separately in the bibliography. Where page numbers appear without a date inside brackets, as in '(89)', they refer to the immediately preceding citation.

1
Introduction

The Refusal of What We Are

As the end of the twentieth century approaches, nobody who thinks about politics can fail to be struck by the enormous changes that have occurred. European colonial empires disintegrated, to be replaced by new nation states. The Soviet system of communist states came and went, inciting serious doubts about the viability of any socialist alternative to liberal capitalism and giving vent to another wave of nationalism. To some, the end of the century heralds the triumph of liberal capitalism (Fukuyama, 1989). To others, those embroiled in and witnesses of renewed ethnic and national conflict, the end of the century looks much like its middle: people kill other people because of who they are and the identities they have.

Michel Foucault is now recognized as a key figure in the intellectual scene of the contemporary West. Throughout his work, he reflected about the political present he lived in, from his birth in France in 1926 until his death in 1984. He engaged in a philosophical critique of the present, asking: 'What is happening today? What is happening now? And what is this "now" which we all inhabit?' (1986b: 88). Reflecting today on our present, Foucault would perhaps have pursued two lines of discussion. Firstly, in spite of all the dramatic shifts, very little has changed. We are still tied to the identities around which ethnic, national and racial conflicts are fought. The same forms of power that bind us to these identities, through a process Foucault refers to as *assujettissement* or subjectification, still operate. Secondly, just as we are bound by the same types of identity, we are also bound in our political thinking to philosophies developed before the First World War, despite their failure to prevent the excesses of politics pursued around issues of identity.[1]

Most of Foucault's thought is posed in oppositional terms. He urges

1

us to 'refuse what we are' (1982a: 216), meaning that we should refuse to remain tied to the identities to which we are subjected. He associated his own project with all those who struggle against the ways in which they are individualized, i.e. rendered into the sort of individuals who they are. For example, he linked his work to prisoners who refused to be delinquents, and to gays who resist their definition as homosexuals. Foucault's refusal to be what we are flows from analyses of the limiting conditions that subjectify us. Retrospectively, he perceives three axes of subjectification: truth, power and ethics (1984b: 351). We are subjects of the truths of human sciences that constitute us as objects of study (such as delinquents) and define norms with which we identify (such as heterosexual).

Foucault's earlier work analyses the limits of the discourses of those human sciences in which various definitions of human subjectivity developed. His attention shifts to the power axis because Foucault found that the conditions of possibility for true discourses about human subjects include complex relations between knowledge about people and systems of government. Human sciences and modern government mutually constitute each other in nexuses of power/knowledge, which Foucault labels variously as discipline, normalization, bio-politics, government, police and pastoralism. Having invested much work in the analysis of power, Foucault then claims that he is not interested in power as such, but in the different modes in which relations of power turn human beings into subjects (1982a: 208). At this point, Foucault discerns ways in which people participate in their own subjectification by exercising power over themselves, tying themselves to scientific or moral definitions of who they are. He refers to this relationship to the self as ethics. Foucault's key criticism of the modern era is that the three axes of subjectification are so closely entangled that the only subjectivities, or modes of being a subject, available to us are oppressive. Under these conditions, we should also reject humanist philosophies of the subject. Refusal of what we are thus entails resisting the truths that human sciences pronounce, the modern forms of government that subjectify us, and even our apparently autonomous self-definitions.

Foucault's political project, however, is not merely oppositional. At the very point when Foucault formulated his aim as the refusal to be what we are, he also proposed an affirmative project, to promote 'new forms of subjectivity' (1982a: 212). Most of this affirmative mood is expressed in Foucault's later work, when he was concerned with notions such as 'arts of the self', 'ethical relation to oneself', 'care of the self' and 'parrhesia'. However, his earlier discussions of avant-garde literature and art also suggest that we can do more than resist our humanist present. Just as Foucault indicates in his writing and life that it is possible to exist as subjects in ways other than those defined by humanism, he also attempts in his work to illustrate how to think in other ways. Thinking and being in ways other than humanist are for Foucault transgressions of its limits that give impetus to 'the undefined work of freedom' (1984c: 46).

Unbearable Lightness and Heaviness

Foucault's transgressive work on limits, which is also the exercise of freedom, is carried out within a field of forces generated by the productive tension between two irreconcilable poles in his work. On the one hand, Foucault is often tempted, especially in his oppositional mood, to depict our present as totally constraining. In this mood, Foucault is a prophet of entrapment who induces despair by indicating that there is no way out of our subjection. He generalizes from present circumstances, suggesting that we can only replace one domination with another. On the other hand, Foucault is also attracted in his aesthetic, affirmative mood to the pole of untrammelled freedom and an escape from all limitations. On the whole, but not always, Foucault resists the magnetism of the two poles, riding the tension by adopting unstable positions between them.

To illustrate the necessity of remaining between the two poles I invoke an image that originates with Nietzsche but has been formulated by Milan Kundera (1984) as 'the unbearable lightness of being'. Life is unbearably light when it has no purpose to it. As Nietzsche (1956: 299) says: 'Man would sooner have the void for his purpose than be void of purpose.' The purpose of Man, Kundera (1984: 8) explains, is given by external and internal imperatives that Foucault would refer to as the power that turns humans into subjects. To be devoid of purpose is to be constrained by no limitations. Such an existence would be unbearably light. On the other hand, a life entirely bound to a purpose that is experienced as an 'overriding necessity' (193), as Foucault claims is the case at present, would be unbearably heavy. The key is to fashion a purpose so that being would be bearably light and heavy.

The most general set of poles to be found in Foucault's work is the tension between constraining limitations and limitless freedom. Between them there is work on enabling limits. On the one hand, resentment of limitations can be overcome by recognizing that we are indebted to our constraints.[2] Lives, works of art and political communities have shape because of constraints. Limitations are, as we shall see shortly in discussing Foucault's reference to Kant, conditions of possibility. However, to accept given limitations as that which determines all that is possible would make being unbearably heavy. Limits are truly enabling when, having given something its form (such as the self), the form engages with its own limits to fashion its own style. Foucault's notion of transgression signifies work on enabling limits. As it is conducted in an unstable force field, the freedom it attains remains undefined.

One of the main themes within which the tension of unbearable constraint and unbearable limitlessness is played out in Foucault's work is that of the human subject. To be a subject can be understood in the sense of being subject *to* something, such as the power of a sovereign. This meaning bears a connotation of being dominated, constrained or subjugated by some force or by limits. In another sense, though, as in grammar, the subject of the sentence is attributed with agency and is thus empowered to act on the object. According to Foucault's middle course, the subject is neither wholly subjected nor entirely self-defining and self-regulating. The subject is indebted to the limits, however oppressive, imposed on him or her for the possibility of being anyone at all, having an identity and capacities to act. Paradoxically, such subjective capacities include those of resisting the power that has made us what we are. However, only under certain circumstances can the subject successfully resist power in a way that does not also reinforce it or reinstall it on another plane. If the resistant capacities of the subject are combined with fortuitous conditions, if the subject works on the limits to which he or she is partially indebted and fashions new forms of subjectivity, then the subject attains unstable and undefined freedom.

Foucault's concept of power also stretches between the poles of unbearable lightness and heaviness. On the side of constraining limitations, Foucault begins with a conventional notion of repressive, forbidding power that confines and excludes the insane. However, a repressive notion of power does not allow Foucault to explain how it functions positively to constitute human beings as particular subjects. Thus, he discusses disciplinary power, which produces a 'subspecies' of delinquents, as positive, though also oppressive, power. On the side of limitlessness, power appears, at least according to some critical interpretations, as an unconditioned or essential power of resistance, as if there is always something, such as the body, that can never be repressed by power. Unconditioned power might also be manifested as an unhindered capacity to make oneself as a work of art, on the assumption that we have a fundamental subjective capacity of creativity. Between these two poles, power is both constraint and freedom, there being no powers that are unconditioned, nor a realm of free capacities. Nonetheless, the interplay of powers engaged in strategic struggle can be more or less open. Foucault's politics aims not for a world without power but to prevent the solidification of strategic relations into patterns of domination by maintaining the openness of agonistic relations.

The poles of heaviness and lightness as regards truth are less obvious. The truths of the human sciences are unbearably heavy because of the price we pay for identifying ourselves with them. To be bound to the truth of oneself as insane, delinquent or perverse is an imposition that restricts the possibility of free subjectivity. Such truths are also entangled with oppressive forms of power, which constitute constraining limitations. The truth is also unbearably heavy in an alternative sense of being necessary or determined. Foucault's analyses of the discourse of human sciences show that the conditions that make it possible for its statements to be considered true consist of restrictive rules. Human scientific truth is then as much imposed, by what Foucault calls regimes of truth, as it imposes itself on subjects.

In contrast, some of Foucault's formulations of alternative truths seem unconvincingly light. He suggests that there might be 'subjugated knowledges' uttered by oppressed groups such as prisoners, which, in spite of the domination of regimes of power/knowledge, have retained the unsullied, crystal truth of oppression. Alternatively, the truth that escapes all limits of power might be what Foucault calls the anti-science of his genealogies, informed by an untroubled 'happy positivism'. Lighter still would be the 'fictions' he claims to write. If truth is but domination, he is not obliged to tell the truth but free to invent a tale of oppression. It would then be a question of choosing, arbitrarily or on aesthetic grounds, between his narrative and conventional accounts.

Between light-hearted notions of truth and conceptions of it as domination, Foucault investigated alternative modes of truth telling. Rather than focusing on the epistemological question of truth, which asks how we know that what we know is true, Foucault addressed the problem of the effects of our will to truth. To work on the limits of truth means, in part, to change those discursive and non-discursive limits that are the conditions of possibility of the human sciences. It also means to work on the limits of ourselves, in so far as our subjectivities are tied to truths of science. The work of freedom might then involve reconceiving ourselves in relation to another form of truth, such as ethical or artistic truth.

Foucault's conceptualizations of thought also veer between lightness and heaviness. On the one hand, thought appears to be constrained by the same conditions as truth, to the extent that someone within a particular system of thought cannot render an account of its limits. Not only is thought absolutely constrained, but without the ability to discern limits, resistance is blind. On the other (light) hand, Foucault in his later work suggested that philosophy and reflection itself could be a way to become free of oneself and one's thought. Operating precariously between these two poles, Foucault's philosophy of working on limits is not an intellectual exercise, but is itself one of the 'arts of the self' that Foucault endorsed. Thought employs the constructive tension between the poles only when it is also lived as practice of undefined liberty.

Difficulties of Foucault's Work

The middle courses navigated between the poles of lightness and heaviness of limits, subjectivity, power, truth and thought, are not easily defined. As a consequence of Foucault's thinking in this indeterminable, fluid space, it often becomes difficult to ascertain what his argument is. He is frequently more concerned to tell us what he is *not* attempting to do, most notably in *The Archaeology of Knowledge* (1972a). Perhaps it is out of frustration

with the indeterminability of much of his writing that many commentators
have tied his work down to one pole or the other, or pointed out the
contradictions between them.

Definition of Foucault's project as merely oppositional has credence as
so much of Foucault's work until 1976 – his studies of madness, medicine,
history of science, delinquency and sexuality – focuses on modern humanism as the imposition of constraining limitations. Portrayal of Foucault
as humanism's permanent and disloyal opponent also seems credible in light
of his 'failure' to develop a vision of a non-humanist world or to elucidate
the new forms of subjectivity to which he is drawn. However, by struggling
to steer a course between lightness and heaviness, Foucault anticipates
the general features of such a polity and of the new forms of subjectivity
which would inhabit it. It is difficult to discern this affirmative potential
because often the middle course is developed in the context of opposition
to humanism and thus often seems to be merely oppositional.

Foucault offers an ethic of permanent resistance. The point is not that
humanism can never be overcome, or that it can be replaced only by
another system of domination, but that any mode of government entails
limits that are apt to harden, tending to become permanent and rigid. This
tendency curtails the openness of the agonistic relations in which Foucault's
'new subjectivities' thrive. It follows that preferred polities are those which
institutionalize the possibilities for agonism. However, even in the best
modes of government and subjectification, the practice of liberty calls for
resistance.

Another interpretive difficulty is that of categorizing Foucault's work.
There is no single adequate classification of his writing according to
academic disciplines, as history, philosophy, sociology, or cultural criticism.
'History of Systems of Thought' was the name Foucault gave to his chair
at the Collège de France in 1970, but that title distinguishes his work from
the history of ideas rather than defining a distinct approach. It is also difficult to categorize Foucault politically, precisely because he was attempting
to think in ways other than those we inherited from the nineteenth century.
In fact, he was rather pleased with the difficulty which commentators
and critics had in defining his politics (1984f: 383–5). In addition, Foucault
examined areas of our culture, such as madness, punishment and sexuality,
which defy the supposedly comprehensive scope of those inherited political
theories (1984e: 375–6). However, it is precisely these difficulties that
make Foucault's work interesting and original.

Author and Oeuvre[3]

The interpretive frame of lightness and heaviness is intended to lend a certain
coherence to Foucault's work as a whole, by locating apparent contradictions and shifts of position within an unstable but recognizable field.

Instead, I could provide separate exegeses of Foucault's main texts,[4] presenting his writing as discontinuous approaches to different themes. Indeed, addressing his work as a whole apparently contradicts Foucault's position on the relation between author and oeuvre (1972a: 24). Foucault objects to reference to the level of oeuvre in the analysis of discourse (139), in so far as it is held to be the expression, in various ways, of the author. He argues that we use certain rules derived from Christian exegesis to demonstrate that a unified oeuvre can be attributed to an individual subject. These rules include consistent quality and style, conceptual coherence, as well as the historical existence of an author. The last is particularly important as such things as the social position, life course or fundamental objectives of the author are used to explain unevenness within underlying unity in his or her writing. Themes of evolution or influence serve to resolve apparent contradictions (1977e: 128–9). It is the unity of the subject's consciousness which is understood to determine the unity of an oeuvre.[5]

Rather than assuming that there is a subject, which invests a whole oeuvre with meaning, Foucault analyses the conditions of possibility for authorship. He claims that authorship is an intertextual position, existing prior to the author's utterances, in which a subject makes statements. This enunciative subject position is defined by legal and institutional systems, including property rights or the different types of authorship that function in fields such as natural science or philosophy (1972a: 130–1). In other words, there are institutional constraints that determine authorship. His arguments here are part of a wider campaign against faith in essential human subjectivity. It is the unity of the individual, the subject, that Foucault considers the most suspicious of the truths which we hold to be self-evident.

Yet there is no need to refuse to discuss Foucault as an author of an oeuvre, as some commentators do.[6] Certainly, there are features of Foucault's work that resist defining it as a unified oeuvre. He periodically offers incompatible self-interpretations about the theoretical focus of his work,[7] criticizes the quality of his former work,[8] contradicts a desire for anonymity (1972a: 17) by giving numerous interviews, and switches between different writing styles and topics. However, all such twists and turns can be integrated into comprehensive interpretive schemes.[9] Foucault's awareness of contemporary rules of authorship should not be equated with success in evading them.

It is characteristic of Foucault and his writing that although he cannot escape the limits of authorship, he nonetheless works on them to construct a problematic relation between himself as an historical subject and his texts. In this relation the oeuvre is not an expression of Foucault; it is not a sign of his profound will, of his genius or intellect. It is in part through writing as an art of the self that Foucault produces himself as an individual who resists current modes of subjectification. For Foucault writing is a technique for transforming himself. What interested him was not the academic status of his work but the changes his knowledge wrought in himself and in others (1988l: 14; 1988s: 263–4). His writing is therefore a practice in which he constitutes himself as a personality who constantly demands of himself and others that they question the limits that have made them what they are.

In this light, Foucault texts are episodes in his autobiography.

> Whenever I have tried to carry out a piece of theoretical work, it has been on the basis of my own experience, always in relation to processes I saw taking place around me. It is because I thought I could recognize in the things I saw, in the institutions with which I dealt, in my relations with others, cracks, silent shocks, malfunctionings . . . that I undertook a particular piece of work, a few fragments of an autobiography (1988h: 156).

Autobiography should be understood in this context not as the narration of the events that befell an historical subject, but as an attempt to fashion the author's subjectivity by writing the self. Thus, the 'major work' of a writer 'is, in the end, himself in the process of writing his books . . . the work includes the whole life as well as the text. The work is more than the work: the subject who is writing is part of the work' (1987a: 18). On this level, of the practice of writing as a technique of self-formation, it is valid to treat Foucault's oeuvre as a unity. Yet it must be borne in mind that this is not a fixed but a fluid unity, not a permanent but a self-transforming identity. Foucault constitutes himself in part through his texts as an agent of change.

Biographical Sketch

Writing was not the only technique of Foucault's art of the self. There were other ways in which he attempted to fashion his subjectivity and to work on its limits. Foucault's life is relevant not only in so far as it illuminates his writing, but because it is also a part of his writing and rewriting. There are already two biographies of Foucault, from which I draw to sketch the outlines of his life.[10] He was born in 1926 in the small French town of Poitiers to a well-established, outwardly Catholic medical family. Perhaps it is significant that his father was a surgeon, as Foucault writes of the political authority of doctors and the medical profession frequently.[11] However, it would be too facile to suggest that his antipathy towards his father explains his analyses of modern government and its subtle cruelty, given that medicalization was only one of the broad strategies of power that Foucault identified. He was a bright but not outstanding student, who experienced his early years and emotional memories under the threat and uncertainty of politics, especially the German Occupation (1988l: 6–7). The personal was always political for Foucault.

He was a solitary and troubled figure during his studies in Paris from

1945, while gaining entry to and attending L'École normale supérieure. He was referred to a psychiatrist, attempted suicide more than once,[12] and for years pondered whether or not to undergo psychoanalysis. Foucault's education was predominantly philosophical, including instruction about Hegel from the influential Jean Hippolyte, as well as study of Heidegger and the phenomenologist Merleau-Ponty. However, he took his second degree in psychology, gaining first-hand experience of positivist, experimental psychology in a mental hospital as both technician and as an intern with an undefined role. Foucault later claimed that the malaise induced by this ambiguous position enabled him to write *Madness and Civilization* (1965).[13] Beforehand, though, Foucault's writing and teaching (at Lille) took the direction of a philosopher of psychology, leaning in both Marxist and existentialist directions.[14] In any case, it was Foucault's deepest personal concerns, his care for himself, that informed his intellectual work.

Foucault, though, had not found his niche intellectually or politically. Partly under the influence of his tutor Althusser, who was to become famous as the leading Marxist structuralist, and partly in the search for something radically different, he was briefly but unorthodoxly involved in the Communist Party. Far more significant was his friendship from 1952–5 with a group of experimental musicians – especially Jean Barraqué, with whom he had a stormy relationship – who were working on the limits of their art. In the following years Foucault practised both intellectually and geographically their strategy of rendering the world unfamiliar. He read avant-garde authors such as Robbe-Grillet, Beckett, Sade, Bataille, Blanchot and Nietzsche in order to think in ways other than Hegelianism and Marxism or existentialism and phenomenology, which were the dominant humanist philosophies. He also took positions as a cultural official in the French Institutes at Uppsala, Warsaw and Hamburg. During this period, until the end of the 1950s, Foucault wrote *Madness and Civilization* as his doctoral dissertation, which the philosopher of science Georges Canguilhem agreed to sponsor.

Foucault missed the political controversy in France surrounding the war in Algeria and the French withdrawal. Indeed, after his return to France much of his 'political' activity centred on finding himself a position, even sitting on a government commission to implement university reforms in 1965. While teaching at Clermont-Ferrand, Foucault published several pieces of literary criticism about avant-garde authors[15] as well as working on *Birth of the Clinic* (1973a) and his best-selling *The Order of Things* (1973b). Up to the latter's publication in 1966, Foucault was associated politically with anti-communism. While this made him a non-conformist in many French intellectual circles, he made no political statements about his sexual non-conformism or his admiration for artistic radicalism.

Foucault's radical initiation occurred in Tunis (1966–8), where, while holding a teaching post, he illicitly aided students opposed to the regime, coming into contact with political prisoners. Although Foucault was disgusted by the anti-semitic pogroms that were part of the unrest in Tunisia, he was then, as he would be later in Iran, greatly impressed by the sacrifice activists were willing to make. Political resistance appeared to be another site for transgressive work, in this case on the limits of power. At the same time he worked on *The Archaeology of Knowledge* (1972a). He was thus out of France during the events of May 1968, when a student revolt almost garnered enough support to break the will of de Gaulle's government and initiated a new mode of unorthodox left politics. Soon after, having had to leave Tunisia, Foucault participated in student protests at the new university of Vincennes, hurling rocks at police on one occasion. However, he tired of all the demonstrations and verbose, factious politics, preferring to concentrate on his work and manoeuvring for his appointment to a chair at the Collège de France, which occurred in 1970. By then he had an academic reputation, a certain notoriety, and much popularity among students.

Foucault's militant period began in 1971 when he was instrumental, in the wake of prison revolts, in establishing the *Groupe d'information sur les prisons*. While the aim was to give voice to the prisoners' protests, the impetus of the agitation came from imprisoned Maoist militants who refused to dissociate themselves from the common criminals. From this refusal and a visit to Attica prison in 1972 developed the thesis of Foucault's next book, *Discipline and Punish* (1979a), that disciplinary power is exercised over everyone in modern society. He was also involved, with Sartre and Jean Genet, in anti-racist, pro-immigrant campaigns, and in the establishment of a new press agency and newspaper, *Libération*, which was to be based on the principle of ordinary people's testimony.

Foucault was no unqualified militant; he distanced himself from the violence of the Maoists and attacks on Israel, breaking with his political and philosophical associate Gilles Deleuze over the latter's support for the Red Army Faction. In 1975, along with the actors Yves Montard and Simone Signoret, Foucault protested against the execution of eleven prisoners in Spain. Networks were formed to wage many similar small campaigns such as support for a falsely imprisoned man. He became preoccupied with the case of Dr Stern, a Soviet Jew put on trial for refusing to block his son's emigration to Israel.

Around this time, Foucault published *The History of Sexuality* (1978b), which was to be his last book for eight years. In his action in support of the Vietnamese boat people in 1978 he declared himself, along with Sartre and Derrida, part of an international citizenry which demanded that governments take responsibility for the welfare of those in misfortune. That was not the only occasion on which he invoked the notion of rights in a political campaign. His support for the Iranian revolution and the Islamic nature of spiritual revolt, expressed while covering Iran for the Italian newspaper *Corriere della Sera* led him into hot water. Yet it should be borne in mind that liberal humanists were opposed to the Shah's brutal regime, and that Foucault responded as soon as the revolution began to turn sour by condemning abuses of human rights in an open letter to the Iranian prime minister.

Chastened by his lack of foresight, Foucault withdrew from activism for a while. As in his militancy of the early 1970s, Foucault found that transgression as work on the limits of power could go awry. In France, he became associated with the neo-liberalism of the New Philosophers, such as André Glucksmann, who had been disillusioned by the failure of post-1968 radical politics. By this time, Foucault was visiting the USA more frequently, enjoying great popularity, and discovering new ways of enjoying himself. Indeed, the focus of his intellectual work shifted away from sexuality *per se* to the more general notion of the human as the subject of desires. His studies of Christianity led him to characterize it as a mode of governing desire by renouncing it,[16] in contrast to the Greeks and Hellenists, who moderated pleasures through techniques and arts of the self. At the same time, Foucault was teaching and lecturing about technologies and modes of government of polities.[17] Only the studies of the classical periods were published as books, shortly before Foucault's death, as *The Use of Pleasure* (1987b) and *The Care of the Self* (1988o). For the rest we must rely on essays, lecture transcripts, interviews and course notes.

Perhaps Foucault's main work in his last years was himself and his pleasures. He had his first, apparently mind-blowing LSD trip in Death Valley, California in 1975. The gay subculture that flourishes in the USA offered him far more freedom and fun than France could. Here he could practise his philosophical ethos of limit experiences, which he had perhaps envisioned in the 1950s, but the techniques of which not even his friend Barraqué had wished to pursue. Foucault explored the anonymity of sexual encounters, the strategic reversals of relationships and intense experiences of sadomasochism, and spoke about the construction of a gay lifestyle on the basis of a form of friendship between men that had been suppressed since the seventeenth century.[18] He was practising an art of the self that was also a work on limits, living his philosophy as life.

More conventional politics were not entirely forgotten. Initially enthused by the election of a socialist government in France, by 1981 the Polish situation prompted him to condemn its inaction, provoking a significant campaign. Foucault remained active in Solidarity and helped its cause through the organization of *Médecins du Monde*, while also developing some links with French trade unions. However, Foucault's work was to remain unfinished. Sometime in 1983 it seems that Foucault knew he would die of AIDS, yet he continued visiting American bathhouses. It is not clear whether he was taking risks with others willing to participate in a suicidal orgy, or was irresponsibly placing his pleasures above the lives of others. Back in France, he used his remaining energy to prepare his last two books for publication, dying on 25 June 1984 amid the accolade that the French intelligentsia bestow on their members. They omitted to mention the true cause of death. Foucault's work on himself had taken him beyond the limit.

2
Foucault's Critical Ethos

Foucault and Kant

The philosophical ethos of testing limits which Foucault pursued on a practical level in his last years was one which he claimed also underlies his whole oeuvre. In a key essay in which Foucault offers a retrospective interpretation of the approach undertaken in his work, he identifies himself with the critical ethos of modernity (1984c). It is ironic that a writer with a reputation for anarchistic, nihilistic, even apocalyptic opposition to rationality, humanism and the Enlightenment turned to Kant as a model for critique. Foucault perceived himself to be writing in a tradition of which Kant was the precursor, always referring to a minor text which was Kant's answer in 1784 to the question: *Was ist Aufklärung?* (Kant, 1959).[1]

Foucault's turn to Kant is also odd in light of the role ascribed to Kant in *The Order of Things* (1973b). There, Foucault charges Kant with having induced an 'anthropological sleep' in the thought of the modern system of knowledge by focusing all philosophy on the question: what is Man? (340–1). Anthropology in this context refers not to the academic discipline, but to humanism, or a philosophy that places the figure of Man at its centre.[2] The centring of Man is a consequence of Kant's 'Copernican revolution'. According to previous philosophy, it was assumed that all knowledge must conform to the reality of objects, meaning that the concepts by which we understand the world must correlate with how the world really is. Kant (1965: 22–3) argued that we have a priori knowledge of objects because they conform to concepts as given by the human faculty of understanding. They are pure a priori concepts in so far as they are entirely independent of empirical experience (42–3). Man is placed at the centre of scientific knowledge, as it depends on human concepts of time and space and other categories according to which the world is perceived and understood. It is the knowing subject who organizes the world according to categories, such as cause and effect, so that knowledge conforms to the subject's perceptions and understandings.

The form of anthropological modern thought that Kant initiates with his Copernican revolution is characterized by Foucault as an analytic of finitude (1973b: 313–18). The figure of Man appears at the centre of the philosophical scene, as a finite being governed by the processes of life, the exigencies of labour, and the structures of language. These human limitations are known to Man as positive, empirical knowledge of Man as an object, yet these positive finitudes also serve as foundations or conditions of possibility for knowledge. For example, we know about Man as a living being only because death defines the limits of life. Although Foucault discusses the analytic of finitude in relation to the human sciences that characterize modern thought rather than in relation to Kant's philosophy, he argues that these sciences function in a space defined by Kant's critical philosophical reflection on finitude (384).[3]

Kant's reflection on limits initially served as an answer to Hume's scepticism which undermined certainty in any knowledge. Kant's response was that scientific knowledge is valid because it is limited by the a priori concepts which humans bring to bear in their perceptions and understanding of the world. The categories and concepts applied by knowing subjects render the world intelligible, yet prevent knowledge of 'things in themselves', as they actually are, unmediated by human concepts. We are indebted to the constraints on our knowledge, which prevent us from knowing the world in itself directly, for the very possibility of intelligible knowledge, organized in such a way that our minds can process it. Although Foucault is highly critical of Kant's analytic of finitude, he learns an important lesson from Kant's reflection on the conditions of possibility of scientific knowledge. Human beings can be indebted to constraints that are also enabling limits or conditions of possibility. Rather than striving to transcend all limits, the critical question becomes which limits to knowledge and life should be resisted or constructed.

Rather than drawing out the helpful implications of Kant's thought, in his earlier essays Foucault prefers to castigate him for closing the openings that a critical reflection on limits offered, by introducing dialectical thought (1973b: 341–2; 1977b: 38). Dialectical thought moves between positive knowledge of human finitude and the knowing subject who transcends such knowledge. The knowing subject is not an object of knowledge but its existence is deduced by Kant as that which organizes perception according to concepts and categories. On one level, dialectical thought mediates between Man as object and subject of scientific knowledge. On another level, it mediates between an empirical, finite being that is heteronomous, governed by life, labour and language, and an autonomous rational being governed by a universal law given to itself. The former is determined, the latter has free will, yet they are both Man and thus the focus of anthropological thought. Kant (1965: 116–26) claims to have overcome the antinomy between Man as transcendental subject and as determined object, but Foucault argues that the two poles of the transcendental and empirical doublet of Man cannot be kept apart (1973b: 318–22).

Foucault took up the Kantian definition of critique as the analysis and reflection upon limits (1984c: 45). He also engaged in his own style of analysis of the limits of knowledge in particular areas under the rubric of archaeology. The term is borrowed from Kant 'to designate the history of that which renders necessary a certain form of thought' (1971b: 60).[4] Archaeology should tell us about the conditions under which certain statements about disease, for example, are considered true and others false. However, as Foucault (1984e: 46) is aware, Kant regarded a priori concepts as 'universal structures' that are relevant in all times and places (1984c: 46). Foucault's stress on the historical and contingent nature of conditions of possibility for human sciences distinguishes his critique of limits from Kant's. As Norris (1993: 56–7) points out, Foucault wishes us to treat Kant's derivation of the conditions of possibility of scientific knowledge as a historical episode. Kant failed to recognize that his own thought must also be limited and conditioned by his historical and cultural circumstances. On the one hand, Foucault's archaeological work describes what he calls the historical a priori conditions of human sciences such as medicine, illustrating how these conditions changed dramatically. On the other hand, he demonstrates that if the conditions are contingent, knowledge must not necessarily have the shape it has. So we could think differently about, for example, health and sickness, or the normal and the pathological. Foucault goes beyond 'the Kantian question . . . of knowing what limits knowledge has to renounce transgressing' by denying that the limits posited by Kant are necessary (1984c: 45).

In Kant's philosophy, pure reason had to be kept within its proper limits in order to prevent it from making speculative errors. As Foucault puts it, 'since Kant, the role of philosophy is to prevent reason from going beyond the limits of what is given in experience' (1982a: 210). One such error would be to claim objective knowledge of some substance or unity called the self on the basis of a mere deduction that there must be a knowing subject in order for knowledge to be possible. Other limits to be placed on human faculties are derived from the division of Kant's critical philosophy into three spheres concerning scientific knowledge, morality and aesthetics. Hence he wrote a *Critique of Pure Reason*, a *Critique of Practical Reason*, and a *Critique of Judgement*. The three spheres require different types of judgements that should not be confused. For example, practical, moral reasoning must be free from empirical considerations of what makes people happy, which we can learn from scientific reasoning. In Foucault's view, the analysis of the proper limits of reason or spheres of judgement is not a helpful approach. Rather than offering a critique of reason in general,

Foucault concentrates on particular human sciences and political rationalities, warning that philosophy cannot prevent political excesses (1982a: 210). Foucault effectively redefines Kant's philosophical critique as a political problem (1984c: 37).

According to Foucault's interpretation of Kant's essay, his attitude to Kant's critique is quite consistent with the latter's account of the critical philosophical ethos of Enlightenment and modernity. Foucault claims that Kant too regards the Enlightenment as an historical event, it being the point at which Western rationality declares its autonomy and sovereignty (1980l: 53; 1986b: 95). Autonomy refers to reliance on reason alone in making laws for oneself. Enlightenment is the moment at which humanity achieves maturity by relying on no authority other than its own reason (1984c: 34). The question, then, is to assess the relation between our present and the moment of maturity (1980l: 53), requiring a philosophical enquiry into the nature of the present. What our present is and where it stands in relation to the Enlightenment makes a difference to knowledge and truth, and the authority derivable from them. We are led to ask 'What are we, and what is our position in our present?' (1982a: 216; 1984c: 34; 1986b: 88–9).[5] Does our present condition enable us to exercise our reason autonomously? Can we rule ourselves on our own authority? According to Foucault this simultaneous historical and critical reflection is the attitude of modernity (1984c: 38).

Critique is essential to this ethos of modernity, in that its role is to define 'the conditions under which the use of reason is legitimate in order to determine what can be known, what must be done, and what may be hoped' (38). Critique is what legitimates the authority of reason as opposed to all other authorities. It is the practice that guarantees that reason remains autonomous. Thus what characterizes the Enlightenment is not a set of doctrines deemed to be rational, but a philosophical ethos of critique, of our present and ourselves, and a questioning about how autonomous we are.

The interrogation of the Enlightenment as an event is drawn by Foucault from Kant's question about whether the French Revolution can be taken as a sign of constant human progress, and whether it indicates a permanent tendency towards enlightenment (1986b: 91–2). Kant's answer is yes, in that enthusiasm for the revolution reflects a deep-seated desire for rational, self-legislated, non-belligerent constitutions. In order to arrive at this reply, he distinguishes the philosophical significance of the event from the dubious success of the revolution. According to Foucault's philosophy,

> the Enlightenment, considered as a decisive event, choice or tendency in human history, becomes for us, as did the Revolution for Kant, an ambiguous undertaking, liable to succeed or miscarry, or to succeed at unacceptable cost (Gordon, 1986: 74).

Foucault redirects Kant's critique of the present to the question of 'how are we rational today, and at what cost?'

The demand to be rational at any cost and to cleave to a rationalist tradition is rejected by Foucault as 'the "blackmail" of the Enlightenment' according to which one must be for or against reason (1984c: 42–3). This blackmail is associated with humanism, which Foucault sharply distinguishes from enlightenment (43–5). Humanism is equivalent to the anthropologism discussed in *The Order of Things*, yet here Foucault contends that it is in tension with the ethos of modernity rather than being what characterizes modern thought. Humanism is defined as a series of themes, or various conceptions of Man that have been adopted by Christianity, Marxism, existentialism and even Nazism and Stalinism. On the reading of Kant's critical philosophy outlined above, attempts to define the nature of Man are illegitimate uses of speculative reason that exceed its proper limits. The critical ethos of modernity does not ask 'What is Man?' but analyses the limits that make us the people who we are, be we normal or pathological, healthy or sick. It also asks whether the limits that constitute our subjectivity allow us to achieve maturity and to govern ourselves according to our own authority. Foucault's analyses of the modern humanist regime argue that we do not, at present, have the freedom to govern ourselves.

Foucault clearly departs from Kant's analysis of limits when he writes that: 'The point . . . is to transform the critique conducted in the form of necessary limitation into a practical critique that takes the form of a possible transgression' (45). In Foucault's version, limits are historical and contingent rather than universal and necessary, and thus are open to change. Critique should therefore have an historical approach, which Foucault, borrowing from Nietzsche, designates as genealogy. The aim of this critical historical approach is to 'separate out, from the contingency that has made us what we are, the possibility of no longer being, doing, or thinking what we are, do, or think' (46). Humanism is, for Foucault, a series of doctrines which tie us to our subjectivities and to particular notions of personhood. These ties prevent us from attaining maturity and bind us to the authority of the forces that limit us.

It should be noted that Foucault's use of the notion of autonomy also varies from Kant's. In the latter's version, reason – which is situated in reasonable subjects – gives the law to itself. Reason is autonomous when it is free from all heteronomous influences, such as human desires and other empirical determinations. Foucault talks of 'autonomous subjects' who are free not because they subject themselves to 'the essential kernel of rationality', but in so far as they have been able to transgress the limits that constituted them as what they are (43). The vocabulary of autonomy and heteronomy is disrupted by Foucault, for whom it is never a question of liberating the autonomous self but of creating the self (42).

Another difference between Kant's and Foucault's critiques is that the latter's must also be practical, not only intellectual. Kant (1959) appears to endorse the practice of freedom when he argues that the public use of reason must be unrestricted. However, he means by this that scholarly argument should be public, but that all citizens must obey the law. There is an assumption that public discussion will demonstrate that the laws conform with universal reason, as in the case of Frederick II's policy of religious toleration in Prussia. Foucault considers Kant's solution to be a 'contract of rational despotism with free reason' (1984c: 37). This contract typifies the political rationality of modern humanism by which individual capacities are subordinated to the enhancement of state power (48). The practical critique conceived of by Foucault would stress disobedience or resistance in place of obedience to current regimes. If Kant's freedom is somewhat cerebral, Foucault's is also corporeal. According to the philosophical ethos of modernity, 'the historical analysis of limits that are imposed on us' is combined with 'an experiment with the possibility of going beyond them' (50). Foucault aims to keep alive the critical spirit of modernity to be found in Kant's work, not his philosophical doctrines.

Foucault and Nietzsche

In contrast, Foucault's work is very close to the teachings of Nietzsche. He describes his readings of Nietzsche in the early 1950s as a point of rupture or revelation, which enabled him to escape a personal and intellectual rut (1983a: 199; 1988i: 13). The intellectual rut was the dominance of Hegelianism and phenomenology in the French academy, with their focus on the philosophy of the subject (1983a: 200; 1989b: 30, 44–5). Foucault held that only a complete break with Kantian anthropological thought could awaken philosophy from its slumber, while indicating that Nietzsche had already aroused it. His understanding of Nietzsche through Blanchot and Bataille taught him about 'de-subjectifying' or the dissociation of the subject through transgressive 'limit-experiences' (31–2). Nietzsche (1966: 23–4, 67) radicalizes Kant's philosophy by expanding the latter's argument that the knowing subject cannot be known objectively. He claims that Kant really wanted to say that the thinking subject does not cause thought but is its effect. It is grammatical habit that leads us to believe that all activity, including thinking and knowing, requires an agent or a subject. Yet Nietzsche (1956: 178–9) insists that there is no 'doer' behind the deed, that is, no subject as such. Nietzsche's thought enables Foucault to detach himself from subject-centred humanism (1984a: 81–3). In the light of histories of contingent truths about human subjects, notions of a self or a soul are fragmented and diffused. The body is conceived as the locus of a self about which so many different truths can be told, but we cannot understand ourselves *as* bodies, because the truths about our corporal existence are also subject to the forces at work in history.

Though the notion of a founding subject may be a fiction, the 'fabrication' or constitution of acting subjects must still be accounted for. As Ansell-Pearson (1991: 274) notes, Nietzsche (1956: 189–92) poses the question of how the political subject who can make promises and enter into social contracts is fashioned. Foucault (1980e: 97) takes a similar tack, by tracing how political subjects are constituted as the effects of power (of deeds) rather than how political sovereignty is established or authorized by the actions of 'doers' or subjects. At least in retrospect, Foucault's whole oeuvre was focused on this question of subjectification, or the constitution of subjects (1982a: 208). Moreover, Foucault drew from Nietzsche a sense that the attainment of even privileged, autonomous subjectivity had its costs. Nietzsche (1956: 190–4) tells us that in order to become a maker of promises, Man had to be rendered calculable through social disciplines and furnished with a conscience through harsh punishments. Foucault's own study of discipline and punishment (1979a) follows the same mood by arguing that these are practices for producing docile yet productive bodies who have internalized the gaze of authority.

Nietzsche (1966: 17–19) was able to arouse philosophy from its slumber by turning Kant's questions around. Instead of asking what the a priori conditions of possibility for knowledge are, Nietzsche asks why knowledge is necessary. His answer is that it is necessary for the preservation of human life, but what matters is not the actual truth of our knowledge, but that we believe it to be true. Humans have a 'will to truth' which is as happy with false as with true judgements, because it is also a 'will to power', meaning a will to affirm life as it is (11–12, 16). Recognition that scientific and moral judgements may be both in error and life-affirming leads Nietzsche to a philosophy 'beyond good and evil' (12). In this philosophy, the claim that truth is discovered is replaced by recognition that it is invented (18). Foucault accepts this teaching of Nietzsche's when he claims that his historical studies are fictions (as is all other human science), whose significance derives from the political effects they are capable of bringing about (1980j: 193).

Foucault credits Nietzsche for his recognition that the political question is truth itself rather than the distinction between truth and false or ideological knowledge (1980f: 133). He claims that his interest in Nietzsche was aroused by the latter's writing on the will to truth and as a historian of truth and rationality (1989b: 61–2; 1983a: 199, 204). Nietzsche's historical approach to scientific and moral reason introduces themes of discontinuity and contingency (1989b: 48, 62), thereby disrupting the humanist trajectory of the gradual emancipation of truth from power. It also undermines Kant's claim to have discovered universal conditions of possibility for knowledge, as these conditions can be seen to change over time and in response to haphazard forces. In his inaugural lecture at the Collège de France, Foucault (1981a: 70–2) describes his own project as a history of the will to know, as it is embodied in specific discourses such as those about sexuality, punishment, political economy or nineteenth-century positivism. In Foucault's version, what is at stake in the will to truth, which distinguishes truth from falsehood, is desire and power (56). Foucault was also inspired by Nietzsche's concern for the will to truth as he perceived the relation between truth and the self (1983a: 204). In the context of the truths of the human sciences and their notions of human subjectivity to which people are tied, Foucault developed his notion of the mutual constitution of power and knowledge.

Foucault also borrowed the term genealogy from Nietzsche to character-ize his historical studies of the interpellations of power and knowledge, and of the different ways in which subjectification occurs. Nietzsche's *Genealogy of Morals* (1956) traces the lowly origins of Western notions of good and evil in a way that denies any original or essential definition of those terms. In an extended commentary on Nietzsche's genealogical approach, Foucault (1984a: 78–9, 86–90) stresses the tracing of the contingencies that effect new interpretations of concepts, morals and rules. There is no original, true or constant interpretation of a concept such as madness, but a series of reinterpretations affirmed by different perspectives. Following Nietzsche, Foucault (67–9) goes further than Kant in pursuing the claim that the meaningfulness of human scientific discourse is not interior to it, but is conferred on it by its conditions of possibility. The way humans interpret the world to render it meaningful depends on their particular and interested perspective. Kant, too, argued that we have no direct knowledge of the world as it really is, but in Nietzsche and Foucault's radicalization, cognitive understanding is imposed on the world. 'We must conceive discourse as a violence we do things, or in any case as a practice which we impose on them' (Foucault, 1981a: 67).

Both Nietzsche and Foucault have evaluative criteria for assessing which interpretation is valid. For Nietzsche (1968: §254), 'effective history' or genealogy must serve 'life'. Enhancement of life refers to the proliferation of heterogeneity rather than to the imposition of a single model of human subjectivity and morality. Effective history becomes the reinterpretation of one's past in order to reinvent oneself as if one were the product of a new past (Nietzsche, 1983: 76). One dissociates oneself from what one has taken to be one's first nature in order to replace it with a second one. The contingency of being what one is opens up space for one's reinvention as someone else.

Initially, Foucault perceived of genealogical validity in more negative terms. The perspective which validates his histories of truth is a 'counter-memory' (1984a: 91). Genealogy combines the intellectual work of the historian who traces the impact of haphazard forces with the subjugated knowledge of those who suffer from being who they are (1980e: 83). Unlike Nietzsche, Foucault identifies with history's victims (Bernauer,

1990: 182). As Connolly (1991a: 187–8) suggests, the solitary hero of self-reinvention envisaged by Nietzsche has no place in Foucault's history of the present in which governmental power has infiltrated so many spaces. It is now misfits such as hermaphrodites who must provide their own interpretation of themselves. Foucault does not share Nietzsche's despair of political action under contemporary conditions, in part because he holds that efforts to reinterpret oneself must resist networks of power/knowledge that constitute subjects.

When Foucault (1984b: 350–1) moves from oppositional to affirmative thought, he turns to Nietzsche's conception of making one's life a work of art. For Nietzsche, life has value as an aesthetic achievement. The key notion is to give style to one's existence by integrating the diffuse nature of oneself into a coherent whole (Nietzsche, 1974: 232–3). For Foucault, a primary feature of the ethos of modernity is the assumption of responsibility for producing oneself on the basis of mature awareness that one cannot discover oneself in scientific and moral truths about subjectivity (1984b: 350; 1984c: 41). Arts of the self are non-mimetic, in that they do not imitate true notions of subjectivity. One thus escapes the tutelage of authorities who define one. In order to do so, one requires the discipline of artists who understand that to create they must impose limits on themselves (Nietzsche, 1966: 139–40). Nietzsche (1956: 256) also recognized the life-affirming value of ascetic practices that fashion subjects. Foucault follows this lead by investigating the ascetic practices of Greek and Hellenist times as techniques of the self.

Another feature of Nietzsche's aesthetics that Foucault adopts is his valorization of creative action rather than Kant's contemplation of what is beautiful or sublime (Nietzsche, 1956: 238). Artistic creativity through ascetic discipline is, for Nietzsche, the embodiment of the will to power (242). Arts of the self are empowering in that one must give oneself style in order to withstand the constant impact of subjecting forces. Yet the task of self-invention is never complete, as the flow of time introduces changes into oneself that must in turn be integrated. For Foucault, too, the relation to oneself as a work of art is a practice of freedom. But whereas Nietzsche practised freedom primarily in relation to himself, creating himself as literature (Nehamas, 1985), Foucault practised freedom personally and politically. His work on the limits of himself was combined with work on the limits of his present, which includes the power relations which subject people. In Foucault's thought, politics, especially oppositional politics, is also the practice of freedom.

Nietzsche's notion of agonism is also central to Foucault's politics (Thiele, 1990: 909). Nietzsche (1954: 32–9) valorizes agonistic contest as constant struggle. The will to power as contest is differentiated from the will to domination as a drive to annihilate one's opponent. The openness of the contest should be sustained by ostracizing any protagonist who predominates in the arena. Foucault translates Nietzsche's ethos of inner struggle to fashion an aesthetic life into a political ethos (Thiele, 1990: 916). This is an ethic of permanent resistance, in which constant activism is required in order to prevent enabling limits from congealing into constraining limitations and to generate new limits that constitute selves and polities.

Just as Nietzsche's heroic task of self-overcoming can never be accomplished, for Foucault liberty is never achieved in a state of liberation but is practised when freedom is exercised (1988p: 2–4). Nietzsche is not willing to forego the will to power which individuals exert over themselves, and Foucault values the 'strategic games between liberties . . . that result in the fact that some people try to determine the conduct of others' (19). Foucault learns from Nietzsche that the hope of a world without power is disabling; what is empowering is engagement in struggle. As in Nietzsche's agonistic contest, the point is to prevent the solidification of strategic relations into states of domination. It is the agonism of permanent resistance that guarantees freedom (1982a: 222–3). As Thiele (1990: 919–21) suggests, Foucault's politics lean toward a radical, agonistic democracy in which liberal freedoms are valued as the necessary conditions for the practice of strategic games of liberty. However, before we reach discussions of Foucault's affirmative politics, the next chapters examine his oppositional politics, which focus on the constraining limits of present knowledge and subjectivity.

3
The Analysis of Limits

The dominant theme of Foucault's oppositional (as distinct from his affirmative) politics is expressed as critical thought. Rather than taking the form of explaining *why* we must refuse the limits of our present, this critique is an analysis of the limits on ourselves. The political critique is articulated in the urge to resist those limits, to treat them not as enabling conditions, but as limitations. Foucault's attention is directed in particular towards the analysis of the form of power that makes individuals subjects. However, before he arrived at this level of critique he also analysed the limits of our discourse, especially the discourses of the human sciences. This led him to concentrate further on the historical and political conditions of possibility for knowledge, which are also limits that subject us as that which we are.

Analysis of the Limits of Discourse

Foucault presents the issue of the limits on discourse in two ways. One is the apparently innocent question of what constitutes the unity of discourses such as medicine, grammar or political economy. The second leads to a philosophical critique of humanism. Foucault engaged in historical critiques of the discourses of psychiatry, medicine, criminology, and sexuality. His sustained attempt to analyse the conditions of possibility of discourse, independent of its context, appears in *The Order of Things* (1973b). There he claims that a set of fields of knowledge

> rested upon a sort of historical *a priori* . . . This *a priori* is what, in a given period, delimits in the totality of experience a field of knowledge, defines the mode of being of the objects that appear in that field, provides man's everyday perception with theoretical powers, and defines the conditions in which he can sustain a discourse about things that is to be recognized to be true (157).

There are sets of presuppositions, which Foucault calls epistemes, that elevate perception to the level of objective knowledge. These epistemes are historical, changing suddenly over time (1981a: 68). To ask 'What are the conditions of existence of discourse?' (1978a: 15) is to ask 'What renders possible the particular historical events of discourse that occur?' (1972a: 27; 1978a: 14). The archaeological historical a priori is also called the 'archive', a 'system of discursivity', that is, 'the system that governs the appearance of statements as unique events' (1972a: 129). Rather than being identified by their reference to essential objects (such as madness), by a style of descriptive statements (such as clinical discourse), by the permanence of the concepts used (as in grammar), by the persistence of themes (as in political economy), a discursive formation can be said to exist when there are regular relations between its objects, style of description, concepts and thematic choices.

Foucault identifies the systemacity of relations between different elements of discourse. 'What permits us to individualize a discourse such as political economy . . . is . . . the existence of rules of formation for all its objects . . . operations . . . concepts . . . theoretical options' (1978a: 9). Rules of formation are conditions of existence for a particular discourse (1972a: 31–9). They constitute a system that enables statements to become intelligible or significant.[1] '"Truth" is to be understood as a system of ordered procedures for the production, regulation, distribution, circulation and operation of statements' (1980f: 133). Yet the rules of regulation of discourse are not only limits that enable the truth to be told, but are also constraints. They govern what may be said, in what mode (scientifically or not), what is considered valid, what is considered appropriate to be circulated in the educational system or another public setting, and who may say what (1972a: 118–20, 14–15).

Foucault's philosophical critique of humanism is most apparent in *The Order of Things* (1973b), where he describes the epistemes of the Renaissance and the classical and modern periods, as well as the discontinuous shifts between them.[2] The modern episteme, beginning at the end of the eighteenth century and perhaps disintegrating by the 1950s, has an 'anthropological' character, focusing on the study of Man. It places at its centre the working, living and speaking human subject. Presupposition of the existence of this subject is a condition of possibility for the episteme, which centres on Man knowing himself in his activities. Man is both the subject and object of the discourses about labour, life and language. Man both obeys the laws of economics, biology and philology, and understands and clarifies those laws (310). The root of the problem is that in the modern episteme 'man appears in his ambiguous position as object of knowledge and as a subject that knows: enslaved sovereign, observed spectator' (312).

The modern episteme functions on the understanding that it can reconcile

Man as subject and object, manifested in three doubles: the empirical and the transcendental, the cogito and the unthought, and the retreat and return of the origin (316). These doubles are basically incompatible conceptions of what Man, his history and his mind are. In his 'analytic of finitude' (312–43), Foucault traces the play of these doubles that emerge along with empirical human sciences. On the one hand, Man's knowledge must be limited, as what we know about ourselves points to those limits. Man knows himself as an object of nature, as a finite being, 'through his words, his organism, the objects he makes', all of which 'knowledge reveals to him as exterior to himself' (313). Yet that finitude, in the sense of the limits of human conceptual understanding, is heralded as the condition that makes knowledge of his finitude possible (314–15). 'The limits of knowledge provide a positive foundation for the possibility of knowing' (1973b: 317).

Yet if human sciences expose the limitations of Man's empirical existence, then what allows him to transcend that finitude in order to know the truth of his finitude? How can 'man's being . . . provide a foundation in their own positivity for all those forms that indicate to him that he is not infinite' (315)? We know that we know because of what we know about how we know. Foucault argues that there is no possible solution to the problem of knowledge, or of Man and his doubles. His critique of the modern episteme which targets its humanist foundation in the figure of Man undermines the claims to authority of discourses of knowledge.

Moreover, Foucault's analysis of the systematic arrangement of the elements of discourse[3] leads him to conclude that the figure of Man 'was the effect of a change in the fundamental arrangements of knowledge'. The existence of Man is contingent on the rules of regulation and systematic relations that constitute the modern episteme. Humanism presupposes the existence of Man, who for Foucault is a figure of discourse which appeared only at the end of the eighteenth century. The startling implication of this is that '[i]f those arrangements were to disappear . . . then one can certainly wager that Man would be erased, like a face drawn in sand at the edge of the sea' (1973b: 387). Indeed, Foucault suggests that the modern episteme is coming to an end, having exhausted the possible constellations of theory available between the three sets of doubles (1972a: 70). Humanism is a failed philosophical project because it takes Man to be its foundation for knowledge, whereas he is one of its effects.

Foucault not only declares the demise of the modern episteme but aims to contribute to it. What Foucault was trying to achieve in his archaeological discourse was his (in)famous 'decentring that leaves no privilege to any centre', especially the subject (1972a: 205). Foucault argues that Man, the subject or the author cannot be considered as the foundation, origin or condition of possibility of discourse. Rather, the subject, and especially the author, can be defined as an element within a discursive field, a particular space from which it is possible to speak or write and which must be filled if the discourse is to exist (1972a: 95–6).

For example, the subject of a discourse such as medicine is a function of legal rights, criteria of competence, institutional relations and professional hierarchy. Doctors can only operate as the subjects of medical discourse if they speak from the correct institutional sites: the hospital, laboratory, the professional journal. They also have different roles depending on the object of discourse they speak about, sometimes observing, sometimes questioning, listening or seeing, which also vary with the institutional site they are in. Since, in relation to medical discourse, we find a variety of subject roles in different positions, it is concluded that 'discourse is not the majestically unfolding manifestation of a thinking, knowing, speaking subject, but . . . a totality, in which the dispersion of the subject and his discontinuity with himself may be determined (1972a: 54–5). Discourses of knowledge should not be analysed as unities by reference to psychological individuality or to the opinions of a particular person (63, 70).

Archaeological analysis thus suggests that the world should not be seen as a projection of human consciousness or rational subjectivity. 'The sovereignty of the subject', has been preserved by 'the search for an original foundation that would make rationality the *telos* of mankind, and link the whole history of thought to the preservation of this rationality' (1972a: 12–13). A transcendental subject who pursues his destiny animates such a history of thought (39). Foucault suggests that archaeological analysis, according to which discourse is governed by its own rules of systemacity rather than by a sovereign subject, endangers apotheosized Man, as the figure that replaced God in modern philosophy. 'You may have killed God . . . but don't imagine that . . . you will make a man that will live longer than he' (1972a: 211). Archaeology heralds the end of Man.

Although Foucault consistently asks what price we pay for telling the truth (1983a: 201), archaeological analysis offers only a few direct assessments of the costs of the modern episteme. There are voices that have been silenced or excluded during the modern era, such as the 'imaginary transcendences' associated with the sensibility of madness (1965: 58). He expects a resurgence of literary language, functioning autonomously, when the figure of Man disappears. He associates such language with avant-garde writers and madness, and above all with Nietzsche (1973b: 382–5). These are different truths which have been suppressed.

The larger costs of the modern episteme become apparent only when the limits of discourse are considered along with non-discursive conditions of possibility, such as 'institutions, economic processes, and social relations' (1972a: 164). To be politically relevant, discourse analysis must address the political problem 'of the conditions of exercise, of functioning, of the institutionalizing of scientific discourses' (1978a: 20). The task of archaeology is to describe how political practice transforms the conditions of existence and functioning of a discourse. Of all scientific discourses, those with the most political relevance would be those 'dubious' ones that focus on the figure of Man (22–5), because their oppressive political conditions of possibility exact high costs from their human objects. It was in relation to those 'dubious' sciences that Foucault pursued his genealogical project.

Analysis of the Mutual Limits of Power and Knowledge

The advantage of genealogy over archaeology is that it includes power relations in the ordered procedures that make true discourses possible. According to the genealogical approach, '"Truth" is linked in a circular relation with systems of power which produce and sustain it, and to effects of power which it induces and which extend it' (1980f: 133). Specific genealogical analyses show how contingently certain rational discourse became true by presenting historical versions of the systems of exclusion that determine what is true or false. The genealogical approach provides historical rather than epistemological answers to the questions of what constitutes knowledge and truth.[4]

Foucault analysed the simultaneous emergence in the early nineteenth century of the modern human sciences and of certain new 'technologies' for the governance of people. At some points all that we are asked to accept is that there is a correlation between the two: 'Power and knowledge directly imply one another ... there is no power relation without the correlative constitution of a field of knowledge, nor any knowledge that does not presuppose and constitute at the same time power relations' (1979a: 27). But the relation is also causal in that it is constitutive (1984d: 337). As a general formula, Foucault's power/knowledge thesis argues that power relations and scientific discourses mutually constitute one another. Foucault does not attempt to systematically break down the elements of that mutual constitution. Rather, his accounts are a deliberate entanglement of power and truth. Power/knowledge is a knot that is not meant to be unravelled.

Knowledge, as human or social sciences, and power relations constitute each other by rendering the social world into a form that is both knowable and governable, each being dependent on the other. According to Foucault's methodological rule of immanence, if something was 'constituted as an area of investigation, this was only because relations of power had established it as a possible object' and power can only be exercised over something that 'techniques of knowledge and procedures of discourse were capable of investing in. Between techniques of knowledge and strategies of power, there is no exteriority' (1978b: 98). Methods of government render phenomena (such as an expanding number of people) into objects (such as population) amenable to scientific study. Simultaneously, scientific methodologies provide knowledge of these objects that renders them amenable to government. In *Discipline and Punish* (1979a) and elsewhere, Foucault describes programmes of government, or models for the rule of society such as Bentham's Panopticon. According to Gordon (1980: 248), these programmes, apart from formulating intentions, also presuppose 'a *knowledge* of the field of reality upon which it is to intervene' and render 'reality in the form of an object which is *programmable*'.

Medicine and the politics of health offer a good illustration of programmable knowledge and reality. Since the eighteenth century, medicine has assumed political significance because of its authoritative role in political programmes of public health. It was called on to ensure the health of populations, and to guarantee the economic utility of the new masses in concentrated urban settings by enhancing the survival of children, reducing the incidence of sickness and providing the conditions for longevity. Medicine also justified authoritarian interventions as part of the programme of hygiene, sometimes gently insisting that parents take constant physical care of their children (the medicalization of the family), at others recommending and implementing schemes for urban architecture (1980g: 171–7). Medicine answers the needs of capital and urban government.

At the same time as medical knowledge served government, power also accrued to medicine itself. The 'surplus of power' that a political programme of hygiene bestowed on doctors included their 'frequent role . . . as programmers of a well-ordered society' (176–7). Capital and government were dependent on medicine as it provided the programmable model of society as a body. Just as medicine considered the human body as the site of disease requiring either therapeutic intervention or preventative hygiene, so did it provide a rationale and a technology for social intervention. The population became the bearer of medical variables and biological traits relevant for economic and political management, once the health of the population was defined as an essential objective of political power (170). Medicine provided the underlying logic of what must be done and to whom, as well as being the bearer of the norm (health and life) which was adopted by government as one of its functions. In relation to political practices with encoded ways of doing things, 'true discourses . . . found, justify, and provide reasons and principles for these ways of doing things' (1981b: 8).

There is also an isomorphism of techniques of knowledge and techniques of power. The means for gathering information which would be considered true are the same as the means for governing the people who are the object of study. For example, the means of gathering the knowledge constituting a medicine of epidemics were the same as those of a policing of populations, the machinery of observation and intervention: 'A medicine of knowledge could only exist if supplemented by a police' (1973a: 25). The unfettered gaze of clinical medicine was the same technique as that adopted by a liberal politics of the exposure and illumination of the social space in the early revolutionary years, when there was 'a spontaneous and deeply rooted convergence between the requirements of *political ideology* and *medical technology*' (1973a: 38). In the early revolutionary period, the political project to discover the true nature of the social body was paralleled by a scientific project to reveal the truth of the physical body. Medicine provided an appropriate technique for knowing the social body.

Moreover, knowledge could only be established as veridical discourse if it could be put to the test by means of social intervention. If social sciences are to justify their empirical, positivist credentials, they need to be able to operate on society as their laboratory and to use institutions of government as their laboratory equipment. Thus, to provide social knowledge, medicine required the institution of public assistance, developed from the pre-modern network of alms and almshouses. Medicine was an integral part of state intervention and supervision following 'a constant, general, but differentiated policy of assistance' (1973a: 19). Only in tandem with this machinery (be it that of the state or private bourgeois organizations) can medicine realize its project of social knowledge, as demography, statistics, educational theories, sociology, and political economy develop (1980g: 171, 176; 1979b: 10).

Some institutions are no more than micro-governments, such as the hospital. In *The Birth of the Clinic*, Foucault argues that the new clinical medicine of the early nineteenth century had been made possible by a series of institutional changes, including the reorganization of the hospital, which enabled it to become the centre of medical observation and learning. What made possible the birth of modern medicine was the 'gaze', a penetrating, tangible observation (1973a: xiv). But what made possible the gaze was the organization of medical space in the hospital that was at once a place for curing and for learning.

Interventionist programmes of power/knowledge also construct objects as their targets. Medicine was the first scientific discourse of the individual, conceiving of each corpse as the bearer of its own morbidity (1973a: 170–2). The programme of public health had a role in the conception of urban masses as 'population', an object which was at the same time the bearer of class morbidity and also of aggregate economic effects relating territory to wealth (1979b: 16–17). Of all the objects constructed by power/knowledge relations, the most enigmatic was Man, especially individual Man. One of the aims of *Discipline and Punish* was to understand 'in what way a specific mode of subjection was able to give birth to man as an object of knowledge for a discourse with a "scientific" status' (1979a: 24).

Let me summarise the ways in which power and knowledge are conditions of possibility for each other. Government and sciences are associated through programmes, which are knowledgeable plans for a world rendered intelligible and amenable to rational management by constructive discourses.

A programme can only operate if knowledge provides a rationale for government at the same time that government is providing the purpose and institutions of knowledge. A science of Man can only pass its test in reality if that reality is already subject to the power relations proposed by science. Practices and institutions that are conditions for the development of human sciences and the gathering of information are also means of government. Power/knowledge is always entangled.

Limits of Subjects

Looking at his work retrospectively, Foucault stated that 'three domains are possible for genealogy . . . truth . . . power . . . ethics' (1984b: 351). The interaction of these three axes determines the conditions of possibility and limits of subjectivity. Foucault offers slightly different formulations of each of these axes.[5] The axis of truth refers to the human sciences which offer objective knowledge about fields of enquiry such as mental illness. Archaeological critique analyses the discursive limits of the truth axis. Power is the most amorphous field, as it includes political structures, systems of rules and norms, techniques and apparatuses of government, dividing practices, and strategic relations between subjects who act upon each other. The axis of ethics involves not only a relationship to oneself, or self-constitution as a moral agent, but also recognition of oneself as subject of sexuality or madness. Though the emphasis in any genealogical account may be on one axis,[6] it is only by taking into account how all three interact that one can provide a full genealogy of any experience or subjectivity (1984f: 386). So, while Foucault put much effort into analysing the relation between power and knowledge, this provides only a partial genealogy of the subject. The relationship between all the three axes of power, truth and ethics constitutes the limit and condition of possibility of subjectivity.

Having so far focused on the axis of truth and its relation to the power axis, I will now accentuate the role of the power axis itself in defining our limits. Foucault explains that when power is exercised and political technologies are deployed, individuals are made into subjects (1982a: 212). Power constitutes conditions of possibility for our subjectivities. Genealogy is 'an analysis which can account for the constitution of the subject within a historical framework' (1980f: 117). Within the scope of his oppositional politics Foucault portrays the conditions of possibility of what we are, of our subjectivities, as constraining limitations to be resisted.

The use of the word 'power' is appropriate to an oppositional politics, in so far as it has implications of coercion, constraint and domination. Indeed, Foucault refers to 'a form of power which subjugates and makes subject to'. However, we need to distinguish between power in its negative sense as constrictive and power in its positive sense as enabling, constituting subjects, even though the forms of subjectivity constituted may not be desirable.[7] Such power (or limiting conditions) produces a subject who is both 'subject to someone else by control and dependence, and tied to his own identity by a conscience or self-knowledge', these being the 'two meanings of the word *subject*' (1982a: 212). The first meaning implies power as coercion and domination by another, while the second refers to the constraint of being limited by one's identity. As the second meaning implies some degree of self-subjection, it indicates how the power axis is related to the axis of ethical relation to oneself. Genealogy thus examines how subjects are constituted by others and how we participate in constituting ourselves as subjects. Later on, we shall see that in his affirmative mood, Foucault believes that we can participate in our subjectification without simultaneously subjugating and constraining ourselves, but the next section deals only with forms of subjectification that constrain more than they enable.

Subjection by Others

In *Discipline and Punish* Foucault offers an analysis of a specific mode of subjection of Man according to scientific definitions (1979a: 24). The mode of subjection is discipline. 'Discipline makes individuals; it is the specific technique of a power that regards individuals both as objects and as instruments of its exercise' (170). Discipline involves a range of detailed, meticulous techniques for the subjection of the individual, functioning autonomously of regimes and institutions and transferable across them (1989b: 170). These constitute the 'micro-physics of power' (1979a: 26). Individuals are formed through training, which is conducted by means of three simple instruments, 'hierarchical observation, normalizing judgement and . . . the examination' (170).

The first of these is often a matter of architecture, of the arrangement of disciplinary sites that enhance surveillance (170–7). Observation allows one to exercise normalizing judgement, punishing all deviations from the norm, including failure to reach required standards, generally by means of repetition of the act that should have been performed. The norm is both a statistically determined standard of behaviour administratively required by disciplinary institutions (e.g. schools, hospitals, armies and prisons), and what is considered as moral law (177–84). The examination is a combination of the two previous techniques. Examples of it include the clinical and educational examination, both of which allow a documentation of each individual as a case, and comparison over time and across the board (184–92). These techniques of discipline are power/knowledge techniques, reminding us that we are constituted as subjects of truth, i.e. as particular categories of scientific discourse.

The particular individual produced by the techniques of the penal system is the delinquent, who fits into a typology of deviancy, as a character who will not, perhaps by nature cannot, conform to the norm. The delinquent is not simply the author of a crime, but a member of a subspecies whose crime can be explained as part of his being, his character, and his upbringing (251–5). Although the penitentiary system was intended to rehabilitate criminals, the recidivist delinquent was not its failure but its successful product. Belonging to an underclass, the delinquent embodied a useful illegality that could be deployed to frighten the proletariat away from political illegalities, to police colonies and to sustain the cycle of police–prison–delinquency (257–87).

Discipline would be of merely local interest if it were not that its 'penitentiary' techniques of government were applicable in other institutions that assumed a carceral character, especially schools and factories. 'The carceral archipelago transported this technique to the entire social body' (298), punishing deviance from bourgeois legality through the power of normalization (308). The more the mechanisms of discipline spread and developed, the less relevant the model of prison became in comparison to the apparatuses of 'medicine, psychology, education, public assistance, "social work"' (306). Each of these apparatuses is 'intended to alleviate pain, to cure, to comfort – but . . . all . . . exercise a power of normalization' (308) by subjectifying individuals either as deviants or as normal. Modern Western society is not disciplined, but it is disciplinary.

Madness and Civilization demonstrates how subjection occurs in relation to an experience 'understood as the correlation between fields of knowledge, types of normativity, and forms of subjectivity in a particular culture' (1987b: 4). Experience, like any other object in genealogy, including punishment, sexuality, subjectivity and power, is not essential and eternal, but has a history (1984d: 333–5). Subjection occurs in relation to experiences and through thought. For example, in the Classical age, madness was conceived as animality, implying that, without reason, Man is no longer human but animal. Possessed of a frenzied anti-nature, this animal insanity represented not natural Man, but the opposite of Man (1965: 72–8).

As a consequence of the subjection of others, of all those like the insane and delinquent who are marginalized by society, everyone else who is normal is indirectly subjected in contradistinction to them. Subjection operates through 'dividing practices' (1982a: 208). Initially, Foucault focused on apparatuses of exclusion and confinement, claiming that lepers in Europe were replaced by the mad in the mid-seventeenth century (1965: 3–7, 38–64). By confining our neighbours, we convince ourselves that we are sane, although Foucault cites Dostoevsky, who asserts the opposite (xi). It is, then, not only the excluded and abnormal who pay the cost of the humanist regime, but all the rest of us who must suppress that part of ourselves that identifies with these excluded others in order to remain normal. We can all identify with this other, which was conceived by Freud as the unconscious and by Marx as alienated man.[8] So, although resistance is most likely to come from those who are most put upon and marginalized by modern government, and who are therefore most likely to refuse their identities (1982a: 212), everyone is a potential opponent to humanism.

The characterization of subjecting power in terms of exclusion and confinement alone proved to be too narrow a framework for the analysis of power. It suggests that power is merely repressive, prohibitive and punitive (1978b: 85; 1980e: 92; 1980f: 139–40). Such power could only ever be understood as a constraining limitation and experienced as unbearably heavy, yet even when power is experienced as restriction, as in the case of imprisonment, it is also productive. 'Power produces; it produces reality, it produces domains of objects and rituals of truth' (1979a: 194). It also produces people: 'Discipline "makes" individuals' (170).

It is in regard to the domain of sexuality that Foucault most dramatically asserts that power is productive as well as repressive. He counters the opinion, expressed by Reich and Marcuse but widely circulated, that the modern West has repressed or concealed all sexuality other than legitimate marital relations (1978b: 3–13). The repression of sexuality reached a peak in the Victorian era, when the interests of industrial capitalism were served by confining human energies to economic reproduction (36). In contrast, Foucault argues that there was an 'incitement to talk about sex' (23) which developed into objective, scientific truth about sexuality (58). Moreover, rather than restricting sexuality to the legitimate couple, the Victorian government of sexuality caused a proliferation of what it considered to be perversions (37). The bourgeoisie of the mid-eighteenth century affirmed itself as a class in its efforts to overcome these implanted perversions, thereby 'creating its own sexuality and forming a specific . . . "class" body with its health, hygiene, descent and race'. The bourgeoisie produced itself as a class-race (124) by subjecting itself in relation to a recently invented sexuality.

The power associated with sexuality is also productive because it enhances life forces. Whereas the paradigm of pre-modern sovereign power was its right to take the life of whoever challenged it, thus being a merely extractive and subtractive power, modern power is exemplified by 'the right of the social body to ensure, maintain, or develop its life' (136). Power is now concerned with the generation of life, which calls for regulation of the biological processes of the population as a whole, or a bio-politics (139). Bio-power deals with social hygiene, rates of fertility and mortality, and birth control (25). The significance of sex is that it lies at the pivot of both regulation and discipline (145). Discipline is a generative power in that it produces docile and productive bodies. Regulation is generative in that it produces a healthy and vigorous social body (147) through its administration and optimization of life (137).

Initially it had been the bourgeoisie that affirmed itself through its sex, which 'appeared to be the source for an entire capital for the species to draw from'. It was believed that if sexual perversions were permitted, the hereditary stock of the class-race would degenerate (118). When, as the nineteenth century advanced, bio-politics was deployed throughout the population, state racism was born (119). The life of the species became a political issue, giving rise to projects for the eugenic ordering of society (149), as well as wars in which whole populations were mobilized and massacred in the name of the preservation of the species or race (137). Life-affirming bio-power may only kill when it does so in the name of the life of the species. Against the background of the doctrine of 'survival of the fittest', racism justifies not only the killing of others but also the endangering of one's own race, as war is a means of purifying the race. Although Nazism is the most extreme case of bio-power, Foucault argues that the play between the affirmation of life and the right to kill functions to some degree in all modern states, both capitalist and socialist (1991: 52–9).

Self-Subjection

Self-subjection centres around the theme of Foucauldian ethics, i.e. the relationship with oneself. It is 'the kind of relationship you ought to have with yourself, *rapport à soi* . . . which determines how the individual is supposed to constitute himself as a moral subject of his own actions' (1984b: 352).[9] Forming oneself as an ethical subject requires practices of the self (1987b: 26–8). These practices constitute 'technologies of the self' by means of which individuals

> effect by their own means or with the help of others a certain
> number of operations on their own bodies and souls, thoughts,
> conduct, and way of being, so as to transform themselves in order
> to attain a state of happiness, purity, wisdom, perfection or
> immortality (1988j: 18).

Foucault distinguishes these from 'technologies of power', but they involve exercise of power over oneself.

When Foucault analysed sexuality and bio-power, he had not yet formulated his notion of ethics. However, it is possible to reconstruct his discussion of sexuality along the lines of his later analyses of ethics. There are four major aspects to ethical self-formation. The first is the '*ethical substance*', i.e. 'the part of myself or my behaviour which is concerned with moral conduct', or the area that is a problem of conduct (1987b: 26; 1984b: 352). Ethical substances include desire, intentions and feelings, as well as sexuality.

'The second aspect is . . . the mode of subjection (*mode d'assujettissement*)

... the way in which people are invited or incited to recognize their moral obligations', be it by obeying a divine or natural law, by following a rational and universal rule, or by fashioning their existence beautifully (1984b: 353). There are many sexual prohibitions that constitute a moral code. Since the Enlightenment the rules about sexuality have existed within both 'a medical or scientific approach and a juridical framework' (1984b: 357), so our mode of subjection follows scientific and legal criteria of obligation to the code of behaviour. There is a *scientia sexualis*, according to which 'the individual constitutes and recognizes himself *qua* subject' (1987b: 6). 'The objectification of sex in rational discourse' was linked to the incitement to speak 'of it *ad infinitum*, while exploiting it as *the* secret'. It is through our sex that we have access to our intelligibility, as it is 'that secret which seems to underlie all that we are, that point which enthralls us through the power it manifests and the meaning it conceals, and which we ask to reveal what we are and to free us from what defines us' (1978b: 33–5, 155). We think we are our sexuality, so in order to know ourselves, we are incited to confess our sexuality to an expert who can interpret it for us.

The particular subjects formed through the *scientia sexualis* were the hysterical woman, the masturbating child, the perverse adult and the Malthusian couple (105). The sexual attributes of these persons were extrapolated to create a whole identity, in particular constituting homosexuality as a species. The woman was medicalized, the child pedagogized, the pervert psychiatrized and the couple socialized, within sexual technologies of discipline, surveillance and regulation combined with new medical, pedagogic and economic knowledges of sex (104–5, 116). It was in relation to all these knowledges that the bourgeoisie created its own sexuality. The science of sexuality may be included in self-formative ethics because the self-knowledge it provides enables self-control and is linked with the ethical relationship to oneself. However, for self-knowledge to be translated into ethical conduct it must operate on the moral level implicit in sexuality's juridical framework. The field of knowledge of an experience must correlate with a type of normativity to produce subjectivity. In the case of sexuality, 'the law operates more and more as a norm' (144), i.e. moral standards are determined scientifically.

The third aspect of ethics is 'the means by which we can change ourselves ... the self-forming activity ... asceticism in a very broad sense' (1984b: 354–5). This is also described as the '*ethical work* ... one performs on oneself' (1987b: 27). In the modern period our asceticism takes the form of 'educative, medical, and psychological types of practices' (1987b: 10–11). The sexual technologies mentioned above are instrumental in our self-formation, but pride of place goes to confession, as the telling of truth about sex. If, in the nineteenth century, the bourgeoisie formed itself by repressing the sexuality it incited through confessional techniques, by the twentieth century psychoanalysis, as the ultimate in confession, provided a class character in the alleviation of repression. In general we can see that if our mode of subjection is governed by a will to knowledge (73),[10] then our techniques of self-formation must always refer to our self-knowledge, both generating it and obeying it.

The fourth aspect of self-formation 'is the kind of being to which we aspire', or the telos (1984b: 355), one's moral goal (1987b: 28). In the modern era, our telos is the liberation of our true selves, of our repressed sexuality, our alienated being, our human essence, or 'self-fulfillment' (1984b: 349). We wish to liberate rationality from irrationality, and to free the pure subject from what represses it into an object. These four aspects constitute the limits of ethical self-formation, which relates to one of the three axes of subjectification.

Analysis of self-formation contributes to a broader social critique. Modern subjection of the insane took the form of an ethical self-recognition. In Tuke's asylum, the inmates were made to feel guilty for the negligence which led to their loss of reason. They became aware of themselves as guilty, as objects of punishment and therapy and as unequal to their keepers, who had not exceeded their liberty but submitted it to the reason of morality and reality. It was through awareness of themselves as objects that the mad were restored to awareness of themselves as responsible subjects, capable of restraining their own behaviour rather than being restrained by the paternal authority of the asylum. 'The asylum . . . organized . . . guilt . . . for the madman as a consciousness of himself' (1965: 247–50). On a grander scale, the definition of European Man, identified with his reason, can be drawn by its opposition to the experience of madness, now understood as mental illness. That form of human self-recognition and type of subjecting thought puts 'in question . . . the limits rather than the identity of a culture' (xiii). We are limited to the identities in which we recognize ourselves as ethical as well as scientific beings.

Governmentality

It would be misleading to suggest that Foucault's discussions of power concentrate exclusively on subjectification. Much of what has been reviewed above under the rubric of discipline, normalization and bio-power can also be analysed in terms of what Foucault calls 'governmentality'. This term refers to the 'contact between the technologies of domination of others and those of the self' (1988j: 19). It refers to the connection between power as the regulation of others and a relationship with oneself. In other words, government is the connection between ethics and politics. One governs one's own conduct, while government guides the conduct of others. Government is the conduct of conduct (1982a: 220–1; 1984d: 337–8).

The tight relation between ethics and power is discernible as an isomorphism of government of the self and of others. The sexual self-government of the bourgeoisie was the basis for the formation of class identity and government over other classes. Foucault identified a similar entanglement of ethics and politics in the discussions about government that developed in the sixteenth century, against the background of state formation and the Counter-Reformation. The former addressed a crisis of political government, and the latter a crisis of government of the soul. In contemporary texts, the government of states, souls and households was interrelated. The art of government was considered to consist of establishing continuity between the spheres, such that a good political ruler would first learn to govern himself morally and his household economically, while a well-run state would teach its citizens how to run their households. Foucault argues that a key conceptual shift occurred when government of the state was reconceived as a problem of economy rather than one of running a family (1979b).

Foucault's recognition of government as a general problem at the beginning of the modern era allows him to supplement his 'micro-physical' analysis of practices of (disciplinary) power with a 'macro-physical' consideration of governmental rationality (Gordon, 1987: 296–7).[11] This involves asking what the purpose of power is as well as how it works. Beforehand, Foucault had located the existence of rationalities, i.e. 'specific regularities, logic, strategy, self-evidence and "reason"' on the level of 'regimes of practices' such as the prison, which constitute 'programmes of conduct', or what we might call micro-governmental rationalities with prescriptive implications. This type of rationality enables one to distinguish between true and false statements (e.g. about criminal personality), and also to develop rules, procedures and means to ends (e.g. to reform these personalities). These programmes of government in prisons, hospitals or asylums were part of a wider disciplinary rationality. 'They crystallize into institutions, they inform individual behaviour, they act as grids for the perception and evaluation of things' (1981b: 5, 8–11).

There are several dynamics at work in the evolution of such a rationality. The most obvious is that practices of power emerge as local tactics to deal with problems of government in specific sites, such as family, army or school, but are applicable in a whole range of settings. This is the process Foucault discusses as the spread of the carceral, the establishment of disciplinary networks and the extension of normalizing power (1979a: 298–306). The articulation of numerous mini-programmes and technologies of government produces macro-governmental rationalities.[12]

The notion of rationality to which Foucault is referring is quite conventional, so it can be explained by drawing on Habermas's (1984: 169–74) reformulation of Weber's account. Technique is relevant to instrumental rational behaviour because it defines the means by which given ends can be achieved. Technical rationalization also requires that behaviour can be reproduced by others who follow the rules laid down by the techniques. Successful intervention in the social world renders political techniques 'objectively' rational. The combination of techniques of government in a programme and political rationality also requires purposive or value rationality, according to which ends and not only means are determined rationally. Political rationalities conceptualize and justify goals as well as means to achieve them, thus defining the proper parameters of political action and the institutional framework appropriate to those limits. They do so through discourses that make it seem as if techniques are addressing a common problem through shared logic and principles. Political rationalities are purposively rational in that, by providing generalized principles, they enable the systematic pursuit of values, the determination of ends selected according to those values, and effective planning of the application of means to achieve these given ends. The combination of technical and purposive rationality in political discourse renders it programmatic, inducing methodically rational conduct which is simultaneously rule-governed, reproducible and principled.

One way of understanding political rationalities as programmes is to consider them as problematizations of their contemporary social, political and economic situation. As such, they regard some aspects of life as problematic, as difficulties that demand thought. When, why and how did something, be it madness, the relation between crime and punishment, or sexual practice, become a problem that required thought? What is at question are all the practices, discursive or non-discursive, through which this something is subject to questions of truth or falsehood and hence becomes an object of thought, be it moral, political or scientific thought. What has to be thought about is how one relates to or controls oneself, and how one relates to or controls others (1988s: 257–8).

As mentioned above, in the sixteenth century it was the problem of government that became problematic. The modelling of government of the state on modes of achieving personal salvation and care of the family, goods and household has consequences for the notions motivating political behaviour. The purpose of and justification for political power alters. Given that the problem was to introduce economy into the management of the state, the purpose of government became creation of wealth, growth of population and health, rather than merely maintaining rule over territory and the subjects within it. If we are looking for the thought associated with this new style of rule, we should focus on new forms of knowledge, sciences of the state or statistics, the science of political economy and handbooks of the continental tradition of police (1979b).

Foucault traced this idea of government troubling itself with the welfare of the population back to ancient Oriental, especially Hebrew, ideas of pastoral power: a devoted, individual, kindly power. Christian developments added the shepherd's responsibility for the deeds of his flock, requiring an individual knowledge of each member, attained by the techniques of self-knowledge and confession, and the obedience of each member (1981f:

236-41). The ultimate aim of pastoral power was 'to ensure individual salvation in the next world' (1982a: 214). Although the pastoral tradition played only a marginal role for a millennium, it reappeared in relation to the two political doctrines of the state from the end of the Middle Ages, i.e. reason of state and the theory of police.

Foucault claims that the modern art of government is the consequence of a combination between the pastoral thinking inherent in police and reason of state. Reason of state took as its aim the enhancement of the state's strength in a competitive framework, relying on knowledge of the state (statistics) to measure its success. It broke with the Machiavellian concern to maintain the link of ruler and state, but was interested in population and welfare only in so far as they contributed to state power. Whereas the Greek state integrated individuals on the basis of an ethical community, the modern state does so by making the individual politically useful to its strength. The care of the individual becomes a duty for the state (1988k: 152–3, 147).

Reason of state relies on the technology of police to make individuals useful. The aim of police is salvation in this world, in the form of 'health, well-being . . . security, protection against accidents' (1982a: 215). The Italian and German idea of police of the seventeenth and eighteenth centuries was expressed in utopian tracts that regarded men's relations to each other, with their environment and in the economy as the concern of the state. These types of ideas became widespread in cameralism, mercantilism and the discipline of *Polizeiwissenschaft*, but were later most closely associated with political economy. Police proposes and attempts to practise a supervision of and intervention in everything, from trade and industry to provision for the poor, from transport and communications to health, from religion and public morals to education. It is concerned with how all these things are connected and contribute to the wealth and strength of the state. Police aims to increase the happiness of individuals, to improve their lives as working, trading, living beings, because the state can make use of what men do not need. Individuals are integrated into the state on the levels of population and society. Individual happiness can be guaranteed only in relation to aggregate developments and general relations, all of which are subject to policing (1981f: 246–52; 1988k: 153–60).[13] In Von Justi's *Elements of Police* the main dilemma of police is presented as the need to increase the happiness of citizens in a way that also enhances the power of the state. This, according to Foucault, is what defines modern political rationality.

Political economy differs from previous forms of police by introducing a distance and autonomy between state and economy. The physiocrats defined society as a quasi-nature with its own regularities which the state should respect, whereas Adam Smith denied that the workings of the economy were visible and therefore knowable by government. Without such knowledge, the economic sovereignty proposed by earlier police rationality was impossible. Political economy offers a critique of government, in particular of the totalizable unity conceived of by police and juridical sovereignty, which is taken up by liberalism (Gordon, 1991: 14–16; Burchell, 1991: 133).[14]

It is through disciplines, normalization and bio-power that welfare can be improved and populations governed. At the same time, these forms of government enhance the power of the state. The integration by pastoral power of concerns of state or collective strength with those of individual life makes the modern state a formidable machine of individualization and totalization. It augments individual capacities as it augments its own power. 'The modern Western state has integrated . . . pastoral power' by reorganizing it as 'individualizing power' (1982a: 213–15). '[P]astorship happened to combine with its opposite, the state' (1981f: 267) at a particular conjuncture in the sixteenth century, out of which arose a 'new political rationality' and a 'new kind of relationship between the social entity and the individual'. Retaining 'the general framework of the reason of state', the political technology of police was introduced into it 'in order to make of the individual a significant element for the state' (1988k: 153).

Is Foucault's analysis of modern power credible? Baudrillard (1980: 88) argues that Foucault is able to describe power so well only because the power he refers to no longer exists or is already unravelling. Bauman (1992: 5, 14) argues that the disciplinary and panoptical power analysed by Foucault is now reserved for controlling those who cannot be governed through the technologies of seduction to the market, about which Foucault says nothing. Perhaps Foucault must pay a price for writing only histories, not contemporary analyses. Yet it may be more fruitful to follow Foucault's general approach to the analysis of power rather than cleaving to its details. For example, if technologies of seduction operate today, we need to know how we are constituted as desiring subjects amenable to seduction. Significantly, Foucault redirected his genealogy of sexuality into a genealogy of the desiring subject. His general question of how we are subjected as what we are can be proliferated to address a range of categories of persons (categorizations by age, by gender, by ethnic group, according to welfare regimes) as well as archetypal contemporary subjectivities, such as the entrepreneurial self.[15] Foucault's analyses of the forms of power that limit us are more of an invitation to further research than definitive conclusions.

Thus far I have attempted to present descriptively Foucault's analysis of the limits of our modern, humanist present. I began by reviewing the limits of discourse, of the knowledge of human sciences, of domains of truth. While some of these limits are discursive themselves, we saw that others are historical and political. As power and knowledge are mutually constitutive, Foucault's analysis of limits is drawn into the domain of power. Power is conceived as the limits on ourselves in two ways. Firstly, power is what subjects us. It ties us to our identities, which are defined according to the truths of the human sciences. Secondly, in his analyses of how power operates and its rationalities, Foucault examines the ways in which subjects are governed, or how some subjects act on others by governing their conduct. These two levels of power can be distinguished analytically, though not in practice, firstly as the constitution of subjects and secondly as their regulation. The analysis of limits so far portrays limits not as enabling but as constraining. The limits on the human sciences, as well as the limits on ourselves, are unbearably heavy.

4

The Limits of Humanism

Foucault's descriptive analyses of the limits of humanism are impassioned denunciations of the modern humanist regime.[1] For example, in *Madness and Civilization* (1965: ix) the confinement of madness is described as 'another form of madness' perpetrated by 'sovereign reason'. The world stands condemned for this act of madness:

> the world that thought to measure and justify madness through psychology must justify itself before madness . . . And nothing in itself, especially not what it can know of madness, assures the world that it is justified by such works of madness (289).

Nor can there be any suggestion that Foucault is a neutral observer of the spread of discipline throughout society, when he writes that 'insidious leniencies, unavowable petty cruelties, small acts of cunning, calculated methods, techniques, "sciences" . . . permit the fabrication of the disciplinary individual' (1979a: 308). Bio-power is even more culpable: 'If genocide is indeed the dream of modern powers, this is . . . because power is exercised at the level of life, the species, the race' (1978b: 137). Foucault is not systematic or explicit about what is wrong with that which arouses his oppositional passion. A great deal of the persuasive power of his work rests on the effect of his language and style rather than the elaboration of normative reasons for resistance. However, it is still possible to draw out from his analysis of the limits of humanism some general principles of criticism.

Discipline, bio-power, police and pastoralism can be characterized as forms of government that are particularly onerous because they infiltrate so deeply and persistently into the lives of populations and individuals. Foucault characterizes pre-modern forms of power as occasional, though often brutal, interventions into the lives of political subjects (1978b: 135-6).

If in the past power had been visible in its exercise by the sovereign, in the modern era it became invisible as the application of power to the individual's body and soul (1979a: 192). Modern power is insidious because of its concealed but effective intercession in daily life, intervening 'against individuals because of what they are' (1988d: 151). Techniques of government and modes of subject are the costs of humanism, but these costs are obscured by narratives of emancipation.

The Costs of Truth

Modern power disguises itself by presenting the truths of the human sciences as advances in objective knowledge about human beings. Foucault denies that such progress occurs, arguing instead that certain forms of knowledge are replaced by others as discursive arrangements and power/knowledge regimes shift. The discovery of mental illness, he claims, cannot be attributed to any medical advance, as it was a function of new dividing practices deployed among those confined in the mid-seventeenth century. Of the motley collection of vagrants, poor, sick, unemployed, criminal, libertines and mad, most were released into the labour market. Criminals successfully complained about being incarcerated with the mad who were felt to be impure, as lepers had been, leaving only the mad in the original institutions of confinement (1965: 221–40). 'What is traditionally called "progress" toward madness's attaining a medical status was in fact made possible by a strange regression' (206).

Similarly, Foucault denies that the breakthrough to clinical medicine in the early nineteenth century can be accredited to 'an act of psychological and epistemological purification' when pathological anatomy was discovered (1973a: 195). What changed, he says, was the way that vision was organized in the hospital. New arrangements that opened the inside of corpses to the gaze of doctors were isomorphic to new socio-political arrangements that opened social processes to the gaze of governors (19). Accounts of the human sciences as epistemological progress occlude the costs of telling such truths. Tales of Man's increasing self-knowledge obfuscate how 'the experience of individuality in modern culture is bound up with that of death', as the individual first became known as a corpse (1973a: 197).

Conventional histories of the human sciences furnish illusions that function as 'retrospective justification' (1973a: 125). Foucault recognizes that discipline could be justified in so far as it rests on scientific knowledge of Man (1979a: 24). Power is legitimated if it is exercised in the name of scientific truth. We have a will to truth because of the 'way in which knowledge is put to work, valorised, distributed, and in a sense attributed, in a society' (1988d: 107).[2] A vast range of social practices, such as economics or punishment, seek to justify themselves by reference to a true discourse, yet should be subject to a politically motivated critique, along with the will to truth on which they rest. 'What is at stake in the will to truth, in the will to utter this "true" discourse, if not desire and power?' (1981a: 55–6.) In producing truths, we produce a rationality that guides us in our government of ourselves and others. It is because 'we are subjected to the production of truth through power and we cannot exercise power except through the production of truth' (1980e: 93) that 'the political question . . . is truth itself' (1980f: 133).

Foucault's approach to truth rules out a humanist emancipatory politics which is grounded in a truth purified of all error and illusion. His argument that modern power and human sciences are always entangled precludes the possibility of freeing truth from power. Keenan (1987) points out that since the Enlightenment we have regarded knowledge or truth and power as opposites. The truth is arrived at by removing all constraints, by allowing the free expression of thought and unrestrained enquiry.[3] Illegitimate power is understood as domination and constraint, which can only operate successfully in so far as it masks itself and labels an illusion 'the truth'. This truth is merely ideology, behind which lurks the real truth. Whenever power is imbricated in knowledge, the result is ideology. To eradicate domination, one must unmask it and tell the truth about it.[4] Foucault rejects this conviction, repudiating the notion of ideology as 'it always stands in virtual opposition to something else which is supposed to count as truth' (1980f: 118). Rather, 'we should abandon a whole tradition that allows us to imagine that knowledge can only exist where the power relations are suspended and that knowledge can develop only outside its injunctions, its demands and its interests' (1979a: 27).

Foucault, however, does not consider the truths of the human sciences to be lies. Truth may not be autonomous of power, but there are truths that correlate with modes of government. The production of truth is 'not the production of true utterances but the establishment of domains, or "regimes of truth", in which the practice of true and false can be made at once ordered and pertinent' (1981b: 9). Each discursive regime is a limited power/knowledge nexus in which there are rules that distinguish true from false statements. In our society the relation between legitimate power and scientific truth is intense, constant and highly organized (1980e: 93; 1980f: 131). This does not undermine the epistemological validity of the truths told about human beings.

Yet more than once Foucault's pronouncements have suggested that he rejected truth as such. Commenting on Nietzsche, he states that genealogy traces 'the history of an *error* we call truth' which is willed within 'the various systems of subjection . . . [and] the hazardous play of dominations . . . [A]ll knowledge rests upon injustice' (1984a: 80, 83, 93: emphasis added). In this light, truth is unbearably heavy, as it is always the product of domination. But must there always be domination? In his analysis of the limits of humanism Foucault portrays the conditions of possibility for knowledge about humans as constraints and assesses that the costs of telling scientific truths about ourselves are too high. These presentations are consistent with his complaint that the humanist regime is unbearably heavy. However, problems arise when Foucault makes statements about power, knowledge and truth in general. If *all* truth emerges from subjection and domination, then resistance would be directed against all truth without being able to affirm truths of its own. Such sweeping formulations are appropriate in Foucault's critique of humanism, but not when applied to all human existence.

The modern humanist regime of truth is particularly confining because moral and legal values are conflated into scientific truth through 'normalization'. Moral–legal norms are colonized by the administrative and statistical norms determined by power/knowledge regimes. In the case of asylums for the insane, the norms enforced by reformers such as Pinel and Tuke were those of bourgeois morality. Even though the doctor's power to cure originates in his moral and juridical authority, this was 'gradually forgotten as positivism imposed its myths of scientific objectivity' (1965: 276). In the case of crime, judgement has ceased to be purely juridical, in that the condemnation of proven acts according to true or reasonable criteria of the licit has become colonized by an assessment of the offender in the light of scientific knowledge of the normal. Not only must the judge take into consideration attenuating circumstances of a social and mental nature, but he or she is only part of an apparatus that may already have judged, and will continue to judge, the individual in question. Such 'judges' include social workers, educationalists, psychologists, psychiatrists, probation officers, parole boards and prison wardens. Legal punishment has become the framework for a care or cure of the individual, legitimized as much by knowledge as by right (1979a: 17–22).

As its purpose is not only to punish illegal acts, this 'normalizing judgement' is appropriate to the fields of education, health and production too (183–4). 'The disciplines constitute nothing more than an infra-law. They seem to extend the general forms defined by law to the infinitesimal level of individual lives' (222). Punishment becomes no more than an extension of the 'right' to supervise, train, correct and improve, because 'right' has become a function of the true. What was a moral rule is merged into a scientific rule, and a normative judgement in terms of right is right because it correctly assesses conformity to, or divergence from, the norm (303–4). Deviations from the norm are punished as if they were violations of the law, which in turn appear to be offences against objectively known human nature. The 'sanctity of science' neutralizes the clash between right and these disciplinary mechanisms in a '*society of normalization*'. As the realm of right and morality is colonized by scientific disciplines (or bio-power) there can be no recourse to right that is not already defined scientifically (1980e: 107).

Normalization causes us to be constituted as subjects of scientific knowledge. For example, the norms of sexuality by which we define ourselves, are quasi-scientific, being derived from biology and physiology, sciences close to the constructed notion of 'sex' (1978b: 154–5). The modern mode of subjection conflates moral standards with scientific norms, so that our ethics are defined by scientific truth. That is why 'recent liberation movements suffer from the fact that ... they cannot find any other ethics than an ethics based on so-called scientific knowledge of what the self is' (1984b: 343). Our present political ethics is irreparably scientific, establishing fast bonds between power, truth and ethics, the three axes of Foucault's genealogy. If there is no available scope for an alternative ethics, there is none for an alternative subjectivity. The axes of our subjectivity are so tightly entangled that the possibilities we are limited to are not enabling boundaries but constraining confinements.

Myth of Humanization

Humanism conceals its costs and presents its history as one of gradual liberation. Foucault first challenges the humanist narrative of emancipation according to which the discovery of the truth about the insane – that they are mentally ill and thus deserve therapy – is accompanied by their liberation from their chains and dungeons (1965: 241–3). According to Foucault, 'no humanitarian approach was responsible for the fact that the mad were gradually isolated' (from criminals) (244). On the one hand, the removal of chains can be credited to a shift in political economic thinking about the value of confining people in general (221–40). On the other hand, the insane were not released from confinement but subject to new therapeutic regimes of intervention and surveillance in a 'juridical space where one is accused, judged and condemned' by doctors acting as the agents of bourgeois morality (269).

A similar argument underlies *Discipline and Punish*, where Foucault tells a different tale to the familiar one of the humanization of punishment, when torture was replaced by imprisonment, the supposition being that the increase in leniency was an indication of greater humanization (1979a: 7, 23). Incarceration was adopted, he says, because of its appropriateness to a new technology of power (218–28). Moreover, 'penal leniency' itself should be considered 'as a technique of power' (24). In itself the prison is more humane than torture, but 'medicine, psychology, education, public assistance, "social work"' along with all other techniques of normalization (1979a: 306), are also more 'humane'. Myths of humanization obscure the motivations for reform and occlude their cost.

Humanist myths of emancipation are yet more insidious because they incite us to seek our liberation through strategies that resubject us. Foucault mistrusts the 'theme of liberation' in so far as it refers 'back to the idea that there does exist a nature or human foundation which . . . found itself concealed, alienated or imprisoned in and by some repressive mechanism', implying that 'it would suffice to unloosen these repressive locks so that man can be reconciled with himself' (1988p: 2). 'The man described for us, whom we are invited to free, is already in himself the effect of a subjection much more profound than himself' (1979a: 30). Technologies of power/knowledge have constructed what we know as 'psyche, subjectivity, personality, consciousness' (29).

Foucault maintains that the self is not a natural, essential entity whose freedom consists in its unlimited expression or teleological realization, but a transitory and contingent result of power relations that constitute it. 'The individual is not a pre-given entity which is seized on by the exercise of power. The individual, with his identity and characteristics, is the product of a relation of power exercised over bodies, multiplicities, movements, desires, forces' (1980d: 73–4). There is no other 'truly' true subjectivity to liberate. Liberation movements are directed against repression, but the notion of what is repressed is derived from the power of subjection. That is the trap of humanism, which binds us ever more tightly to our subjectivities through our efforts to liberate ourselves.

This trap is presented in Foucault's reversal of the repressive hypothesis, a Freudian-Marxist belief that we can liberate ourselves by liberating our sexuality, which is held to be the core of our subjectivity. According to Foucault, bio-power ties us to our sexual identities, leading us to believe that we are our sexuality. In general bio-power aims to optimize all human life forces, such as libido, yet resistance to it is posed in terms of the same life forces that bio-power targets. Against the power over life there are struggles for 'the "right" to life, to one's body, to health, to happiness, to the satis-faction of needs, and beyond all "alienations", the "right" to rediscover what one is and all that one can be' (1978b: 145). If one believes one is one's sexuality, then struggle takes the form of anti-repression. Yet such revolu-tion is 'nothing more, but nothing less . . . than a tactical shift and reversal' (131). Ironically, we believe that our liberation is at stake (159).

Humanist political rationality contributes to this entrapment because it is based on an antinomy of totalization and individualization. The struggle for freedom of individuals in the West has taken the form of the 'acquisition of capabilities'. Initially conceived as a fight for greater autonomy, this struggle has been accompanied by the development of political technologies, disciplines and normalization processes (1984c: 47–8). These practices and techniques of government subjectify the supposedly free or to-be-freed subject. The state has built its strength not only by paying attention to the totality of its resources but by enhancing the potential of every individual under its auspices (1982a: 213–4). Modern pastoral government invests in the capacities of the individual, developing qualities of rationality, autonomy and decision making. It also invests in capacities that are thought to escape rational confines: the body, spontaneity, creativity and the libido. Foucault ascribes the 'failure' of our political theories to 'the fact that this integration of individuals in a community or in a totality results from a constant correlation between an increasing individualization and the reinforcement of this totality' (1988k: 161–2). The perversity of modern humanism is that the more Promethean we become, the more Sisyphian are our efforts.

The antinomy of humanism also appears as the clash between 'law and order' (1988k: 162), or what is by now familiar to us as the difference between right and norm. As juridical subjects, we are invested with rights that respect us as the possessors of rationality, autonomy and free will. We fulfil ourselves by realizing these qualities. The basis of order, however, is that normal individuals behave rationally and autonomously, thus requiring a minimum of coordination by government. By establishing a symmetry between the fulfilment of subjectivity and social order, modern political rationality ensnares us in its subjecting embrace. Under these circumstances, the state's order always supersedes the individual's fulfilment.

Enhancement of subjectifying power is not matched by an equivalent degree of individual empowerment. '[H]umanism is everything in Western civilization that restricts *the desire for power*' (1977i: 221). If power is, as Foucault understands it, a positive, constitutive relation, then the restriction of the desire for power refers to the unwillingness to take responsibility for one's own subjectification. Humanism seems to endow us with every power of agency except for agency with respect to ourselves. Foucault denounces humanism as

> the totality of discourse through which Western man is told: 'Even though you don't exercise power, you can still be ruler. Better yet, the more you deny yourself the exercise of power, the more you submit to those in power, then the more this increases your sovereignty' (1977i: 221).

The rulers and sovereigns of humanism are a series of 'pseudo-sovereignties':

> consciousness (sovereign in a context of judgement, but subjected to the necessities of truth), the individual (a titular control of personal rights subjected to the laws of nature and society), basic freedom (sovereign within, but accepting the demands of an outside world and 'aligned with destiny') (221).

What maintains the sovereignty of the subject (truth, right, destiny) lies beyond the subject itself, but these very things that uphold the subject are derived from the subject. We are subject to Human Truth, to Human Right, to Human Destiny. Humanism offers justice, liberty, equality and community to these pseudo-sovereign subjects, not to us.

The antinomy of humanism is also the double bind of the subject. 'The theory of the subject (in the double sense of the word) is at the heart of humanism' (1977i: 222). One can be a political subject of a state or sovereign, and therefore subject to power and the rule of another. There is also the grammatical subject of a sentence, attributed with agency and the capacity to rule others.[5] The double bind of humanism posits subjects who are always subject to something else, such as the law (1988i: 14). On the side of totality in the humanist antinomy are 'unreal', transcendent or metaphysical subjects, in the form of Truth, Right and Destiny. To paraphrase Foucault, the sovereign of humanism is never us, it is never you or I. Eluding us in the double play between subject and truth, subject and value, subject and destiny, the transcendent subject is our sovereign. So it is not we who can tell the Human Truth, nor we who can discern Human Right from wrong, nor we who can direct Human Destiny in history. We are their subjects, and in order to retain or expand our subjectivity, which is all we are, we must accept their sovereignty. That is why humanism must be refused.

Prophet of Entrapment?

Does Foucault's portrayal of humanism negate the purpose of resistance to it by suggesting that we cannot escape its trap? Can we resist the constraining limits of humanism, or are we bound to *'perpetual spirals of power and pleasure'* (1978b: 45)? Does genealogy teach us that the whole of history is 'a single drama' of 'the endlessly repeated play of dominations'? Is Foucault's lesson that we are trapped for eternity as 'humanity ... proceeds from domination to domination' (1984a: 85)? That would be the case if his indictment of the particularly constraining limits of humanism were applied to the whole of history. His narrative would be 'the story of freedom endlessly snatched at and denied' (Cocks, 1989: 70), or even more pessimistically, a teleology of increasing subjection (Meisel, 1979: 240).

Up to and including *The History of Sexuality*, Foucault analyses conditions of possibility of subjectivity as limitations, directing his oppositional politics against these conditions and their costs. Genealogies of the modern subject reveal that the three axes of subjection – power, truth and ethics – are so constrictively intertwined that even projects of liberation succeed only in rearranging the form of subjection. In the modern humanist regime, being is unbearably heavy. The power which seems to have turned us into objects, repressed our potential and alienated us from our true being is the same power that has subjected us as those selves whom we wish to liberate. We embrace our given subjectivities because they promise our liberation through the overcoming of power. Yet, power pursues the same programmes that we do, i.e. our salvation through welfare or revolution, or the affirmation of our lives. That is why we must refuse to be what we are: because if we fight to be what we truly are, we will not dismantle our confinements, merely rearrange them; because the enabling limits of that which we are constrain us to remain what we are unless we can resist the limits; because to accept what we are means to accept subjection. Foucault's oppositional politics is posed in substantially negative terms. There is no plea here for new subjectivities, but a critique of the contemporary subject and its conditions of possibility.

One does not need to be excessively biased in one's selections of Foucault's texts to be able to represent him as an almost entirely oppositional political thinker. Rather than attempting to provide political answers, Foucault wishes to 'question politics' along lines that 'are not determined by a preestablished political outlook and do not tend toward the realization of some definite political project' (1984e: 375). He is interested in challenging what exists, not proposing alternatives (1981b: 13). When faced with the 'tiresome question' of 'what replaces the system?', Foucault responds 'that to imagine another system is to extend our participation in the present system' (1977i: 230). Attempts to establish alternative institutions such as free universities or people's courts are doomed to fail as they are soon 'reabsorbed by the dominant structure' (232). If efforts at resistance are not coopted they are only temporarily successful: 'We strike and knock against the most solid obstacles; the system cracks at another point; we persist. It seems that we're winning, but then the institution is rebuilt; we must start again' (1977i: 230). The struggle against humanist subjectification seems to be an endless, ongoing series of skirmishes and battles in a war that can never ultimately be won. The reaction to complete entrapment would be despair.

Foucault does not despair, but asks 'How can the growth of capabilities be disconnected from the intensification of power relations?' (1984c: 48). How can we escape the antinomy of humanism, whereby every empowerment of individual subjects is matched by the growth of subjectifying capacities of government? How can we affirm new forms of subjectivity? In order to adopt this affirmative position he must address subjectification or the constitution of subjects not only as subjection but as empowerment of individuals who are active subjects. It is contemporary forms of subjectivity that are to be resisted, and present identities to which we should refuse to be tied. We can therefore strive for alternative modes of subjectivity (1982a: 216). In general, Foucault must cease to depict being, and even modern humanist regimes, as unbearably heavy. He must extend the analysis of limits from one of their costs and constraints to one of their benefits and enablements. Before we move on to the affirmative mood in Foucault's thought, we will turn to his critique of political philosophy, which centres on its implication in the power relations it claims to regulate.

5

Foucault's Regicide of Political Philosophy

Political Philosophy as Critique

Kant's three critiques of pure reason, practical reason and judgement establish the proper limits for the use of these three faculties. His philosophical task is to prevent excesses of reason and judgement. Foucault conceives of political philosophy along Kantian lines, as a philosophical project to determine the proper limits of political power:

> we can formulate the traditional question of political philosophy in the following terms: how is the discourse of truth, or quite simply, philosophy as that discourse which *par excellence* is concerned with truth, able to fix limits to the rights of power? (1980e: 93)

Foucault does not refer to scientific truth, but to a philosophical truth which is assumed to have its own force. Political philosophy is the discourse that distinguishes the excesses of humanist regimes from their legitimate limits. It is 'concerned with justifying the right way or ways and identifying the wrong ways in which political power is to be exercised' (Plant, 1991: 2).

Political philosophy also critiques the limits of power in its role as the discourse of legitimation. Political theory, argues Habermas (1979: 178–81), legitimizes political orders by demonstrating that they are right or just. Political orders may be considered legitimate because they are an authentic reflection of a society's self-understanding of its moral motivations.[1] They may also be justified ontologically, that is as systems appropriate to theoretical knowledge or belief about human nature and worldly reality.[2] Habermas (1979: 184, 188) himself insists that the only forms of valid legitimation in the contemporary era are self-reflective, being derived from the conditions and procedures by which rational agreement can be reached by free and equal persons.[3] Whatever form legitimating political theory takes, however, it makes claims that are supposed to be rational, objective and inter-subjectively valid (Plant, 1991: 2–3). Political theory is understood as a special type of knowledge that regulates power (Walzer, 1989: 209).

Foucault claims that it is the term 'right' which is supposed to define the proper limits of power (1980e: 95). The questions posed traditionally are whether the sovereign power has the right to do what it does (such as taking life), or whether subjects have rights which the sovereign power may not violate (such as the right to life). Political theory remains tied to the notion of sovereignty, which becomes democratic and collective by being transferred from the monarch to the people (1980e: 105). Yet we are still faced with the same issues of why we ought to obey the law and the legitimacy of the use of power. Doctrines of sovereignty have survived since feudal times to serve absolutism, opposition to it, and notions of popular sovereignty on which parliamentary democracy is based. As these questions are always framed in legal terms, Foucault refers to such political theory as a 'juridico-discursive' theory of power (1978b: 82). He also repudiates the whole juridico-discursive tradition of political theory: 'what we need . . . is a political philosophy that isn't erected around the problem of sovereignty . . . We need to cut off the King's head: in political theory that has still to be done' (1980f: 121). This is Foucault's regicide of political theory.

The king's head may not be as firmly on his shoulders as Foucault believes. His analysis is more appropriate to the French model, where republican state sovereignty replaced a monarchical one, than to the United States. In the American model, ultimately rights remain with the individual, while political authority is divided between various branches of government that check and balance each other, rather than being ensconced in a single authority embodying the sovereignty of the people. When sovereignty is fragmented, liberal political philosophy must confront more problems than the legitimate limits of government interference or of individual free action. The key problem becomes the reconcilability of individual liberty with social order and cohesion. How can anarchy be prevented if each individual is king? Foucault's overly schematic and reductive presentation of political philosophy as a discourse of sovereignty overlooks, among others, such liberal discussions.

Foucault has a stronger case when he relates to the connection between political philosophy and sovereign power as a supposedly neutral arbiter. Monarchy presented itself as the neutral arbiter, the law, which can settle all the social disputes that endanger order. By determining what was within the rights of, and what was prohibited for, others, this sovereign personage appeared to be indispensable, while the power it exercised seemed to be judicial and fair (1980f: 121). The regulatory role of determining the proper limits of power, initiated by the monarch, continued by jurists and claimed by political philosophers, can thus be said to be a function of the sovereign. By assuming the mantle of sovereignty, political philosophy asserts its privilege as a discourse above the fray of political dispute with the authority to judge where power is used illegitimately. Foucault argues that neither sovereign power nor political philosophy are neutral arbiters.

Yet all political theory that claims to legitimate political order has to portray itself as external to the system it judges. In this sense, all political philosophy is foundationalist in a weak sense. Foundationalism can be defined as a belief that 'any political justification worthy of the name must be grounded on principles that are (1) undeniable and immune to revision and (2) located outside society and politics' (Herzog, 1985: 20).[4] Perhaps no political theory can fulfil the first criterion, but political theories do rely, at least in part, on extra-political claims and grounds. This is most apparent when theories appeal to human nature or to reason. Even communitarian theories, which allegedly articulate principles underlying the practices of their communities, rely on extra-communal claims. Communitarians must decide who belongs to the community and who should be excluded, which would require an extra-communal knowledge of its boundaries. In Foucault's terms, what enables the identity of a community to be defined is political practices of subjection, rather than deep self-awareness.[5]

Political philosophy claims that as a neutral, universal, true discourse it is 'outside power, or ... the reward of free spirits' (1980f: 131). Foucault countered these assertions by referring to an alternative tradition of historical political theory from the seventeenth century which viewed the supposedly neutral law of the monarchy as the inscription of the right of the victor. In the English case the 'universal truth and general right' expressed by the law were regarded by theorists such as Coke as 'illusions or traps' disguising the 'Norman yoke' to which the free native Saxons had been subjected since the conquest of 1066. The sovereignty of rational law was established only when the din of battle was silenced, when 'the blood ... [had] dried on the codes of law'. This tradition was articulated again in the nineteenth century in discourses of class and racial struggle (1979c: 16–19).[6]

Just as the authority of the truth of the human sciences rests on its concealment of its entanglement with power, so does that of political theory. Foucault describes the integration of these two types of true discourse as normalization. Recall that legal notions of rights are colonized by the scientific norms deployed in strategies of government, while the latter rely on the moral authority of the former to extend themselves without provoking much opposition. As a result, even when we believe we are upholding our sovereign rights against the state or the encroachments of disciplinary power, we do so in the name of a right and through a juridical system that has itself been disciplined (1980e: 105–7). It is thus ultimately self-defeating to attempt to oppose discipline and normalization by recourse to the language of rights and sovereignty. In so far as political theory grounds itself in judicial rights and moral values, it is as enmeshed in power relations as are the human sciences. Rather than adjudicating the limits of power from outside politics, it is, like any other truth, 'a thing of this world' (1980f: 131). Political theory has no extra-political foundations on which to stand.

In some essays, Foucault makes unjustifiably strong claims against political philosophy. He asserts that by continuing to discuss norms as if they are rights, political philosophy masks, conceals and effaces the dominative operations and effects of modern, normalizing power. It is the super-imposition of a system of right on the mechanisms of discipline that makes power tolerable. The theory of sovereignty has functioned, throughout the modern era, as an ideology (1978b: 86; 1980e: 95, 105–6). Juridical political discourse is misleading, giving us the impression that our political life really is governed by laws of right, whereas the rules that govern us are actually norms of human behaviour. Foucault overstates his case here as he would have to assert that his account is true whereas all others are false. He wishes to avoid assuming this position (1980f: 118), as it entails an unwarranted claim that his writing escapes all power/knowledge regimes.

A somewhat weaker complaint raised by Foucault is that juridico-discursive political theory is irresponsible because it relies on a model of power as negative, prohibiting excesses of the right to power or infringements of rights to be protected from power. Foucault considered such negative notions of power to be inadequate and misleading. Indeed, Foucault often accentuates analytic and descriptive treatments of power in political philosophies rather than the normative limits they attempt to place on power, because his main project is to 'construct an analytics of power that no longer takes law as a model' (1978b: 90), rather than to develop 'a new form of right . . . liberated from the principle of sovereignty' (1980e: 108). Foucault's criticisms are misplaced here to some extent. We might demand of political philosophies that they draw on adequate analyses of the power whose proper limits they are supposed to define; but political philosophies more commonly draw on analytical theories of power than develop them. This level of critique is also too dismissive of other political theories, such as Marxism, which Foucault argues also rely on negative conceptualizations of power (88–9).

Foucault states that although it is banal to point out that philosophy is unable to restrain excesses of power, such banality indicates the problematic relation between power and rationality (1982a: 210). Neither reason in general nor a global concept of rationalization can be blamed for political excess, yet reason as philosophical critique is unable to perform its ascribed task of defining the proper limits of power. Instead, we should look to the links between particular rationalities which operate in specific spheres, such as sexuality and crime (1982a: 210). On this level the excesses of humanism might be resisted, not by limiting it, but by uprooting its rationality: 'Liberation can only come from attacking ... political rationality's very roots' (1981f: 254).

Political Theories as Governmental Rationalities

Political Thought and Rationality

A critique of political thought is crucial to Foucault's oppositional politics. Power relations between people, or the ways we govern ourselves and others, involve certain types of rationality. A crucial feature of his analysis is his insistence that because rationality is always implicated in practical power relations, it is plural rather than unified. There are no 'more or less perfect forms of rationality' but only 'forms of rationality [that] inscribe themselves in practices' (1981b: 8). '[T]hose who resist or rebel against a form of power cannot merely be content to denounce violence or criticize an institution.' They must be able to recognize and challenge the particular form of rationality whose logic justifies such violence and organizational procedures (1981f: 254).

A Foucauldian critique of political thought rests on the assumption that thought has a material effect on government. Rationalization of government does not mean that a logical facade is affixed to unconsidered practices in order to justify it. Rather, practices 'rest' on 'modes of thought', which 'thought ... is often hidden, but ... always animates everyday behavior. There is always a little thought even in the most stupid institutions' (1988h: 154–5). Thought, for Foucault, is not something superfluous, a superstructural reflection of social reality. 'Thought exists independently of systems and structures of discourse' (155). Thought is an integral aspect of action, because when we do, speak, behave, we do so in relation to thought.

Thought is not independent of but is complexly related to economic, social and political determinations, so there are events of thought just as there are historical events (1984d: 334–5).[7] Thought is materialized in discourse, which has 'conditions of existence and rules of formation' (1978a: 24). Hence, thought's dependence on practice must also be recognized. The 'freedom' and neutrality of thought are limited not only by material conditions but also by discursive rules about what is accepted as 'political philosophy'. Discourse also has material effects on practice, problematizing fields of experience, then rendering them programmable in thought.

As part of an oppositional politics, Foucault analyses the constraining limitations of political rationality in order to 'think differently' about the experiences and problems addressed by these rationalities (1987b: 9).

Foucault refuses to follow any 'preestablished political outlook' or a 'definite political project' (1984e: 375). When Foucault questions politics, he refers to political thought and discourse. He examines how it responds to certain problems and the reasons it gives for its responses (1984f: 385). So he is not only interested in the practices developed to deal with madness, crime and sexuality, but also in the thought that guides or justifies these solutions. Responses to such apparently marginal issues involve power relations and practices of government that extend beyond their specific field (such as the disciplining of society) and whose rationale must be interrogated (1981f: 254). If we want to uncover all the thought behind the rules that govern our collective life, we should address the discourses of knowledge consisting of the human sciences, which are accounts of the disciplinary techniques according to which we are governed.

In Foucault's view, conventional political philosophy, with its talk of sovereignty and rights, diverts us from the political thought which underlies government (1980e: 106). We are given the impression that society functions because of a social contract, whereas it is discipline that constitutes the social fabric. While 'philosophers and jurists' had a 'dream of a perfect society' based on a 'primal social contract', there was also 'a military dream of society' based on national discipline (1979a: 169). These dreams may be schemes for the government of a city under plague (198–9), or the simple architectural paradigm of Bentham's Panopticon for the government of institutions. Discourses such as mercantilism, cameralism, *Polizeiwissenschaften* and political economy contain more of such operative political rationalities than does political philosophy.[8] It is only with the addition of all these discourses that we would have a full account of the thought directing our politics.

However, a full account of political thought cannot be restricted to the cognitive features of power/knowledge regimes. To do so would be to overlook the purposive rationality which directs the instrumental rationality of government. Such an account must both address concealed or unconsidered levels of political rationality and analyse conventional political philosophies as rationalities.

Liberalism

The only political philosophy that Foucault analyses as a political rationality is liberalism.[9] This may be because, as Foucault understands it, liberalism is a critique of power and thus the paradigmatic political philosophy. Foucault defines liberalism as 'a practice (*pratique*), that is, as a "way of doing" which is directed toward goals and which regulates itself by means of a continuing reflection'. Beginning with a basic respect for individual rights and the liberty of action, it arrives at the principle that 'there is always too much government', and sets itself the problem of why there has to be government at all, and if there must be, what the legitimate limits of its activity are (1981d: 354–5). In order to perceive the problem, liberalism had to assume the existence of society, an entity with its own goals and regularities existing independently of the state, as suggested by the scientific discourse of political economy. According to the previous rationalities, the ordered functioning of economy, populations, family life – of what came to be known as society – depended on government intervention. Instead of asking what is the best form of government for the state to achieve its goals, liberalism asks how government must be limited if society is to attain its goals (1981d: 354–6; 1984g: 242).

Liberalism serves both as justification of minimalist government, which allows maximal scope for the economy, and as a critique of excessive government, which could be gauged according to its disruptive effect on the market. On the whole, the most appropriate technology for liberal government is legal, defining limits of government action and legislating intervention when representatives of the governed feel it is necessary. Foucault's analysis focuses on 'the types of rationality which are put into operation in the procedures through which a state administration directs the conduct of men' (1981d: 358). It is an analysis of 'real' or 'actually existing' liberalism (Gordon, 1991: 18).[10]

Foucault explains the shift from police to liberalism by arguing that in earlier periods and less cohesive societies, disciplinary police was necessary to constitute the socio-political body. The disciplined individual recognized himself as one of the 'meticulously subordinated cogs' of a social machine (1979a: 169). 'Discipline is a political anatomy of detail', and it was by paying attention to each individual, to each detail, that Napoleon wanted to encapsulate society as a vast machine (139–41). Once society had been constructed as a self-regulative machine, the disciplines appeared to be 'a cumbersome form of power' (1980c: 58). According to liberal critique, public authority could not possess the detailed knowledge to legislate for every possibility. One of the principles of liberal government was to economize state activity, so the 'disciplinarization' of the state took the form of a surveillance of state activity (Gordon, 1991: 24–7).[11]

Foucault does not suggest that cohesion is simply taken for granted by liberals, but focuses on those liberals who do not accept the supposed cohesiveness of a social contract.[12] The British empirical philosophers, particularly Hume, Smith and Ferguson, claimed that rather than there being a juridical subject of rights, there is an economic subject of interests who, as the bearer of arbitrary and irrenouncable interests, could never agree to the restrictions of a social contract. It is the unruliness and heterogeneity of this subjectivity that precludes sovereignty over the economic sphere (Gordon, 1991: 21–2; Burchell, 1991: 137).

Government and social cohesion are nonetheless possible because of centripetal forces that countervail economic centrifugality. These forces are forms of natural sympathy or human sociability whereby society is always organizing itself, dividing political labour according to leadership skills and formalizing the division legally. Economic Man is objectified and rendered governable as he is also natural-social Man, an economic egoism situated in social bounds. Government is a social demand for the degree of order necessary as a condition for the self-government of the 'natural' processes of society and economy. To ensure that government follows the requirements of these processes, interested subjects participate both in legislation and scrutiny of government activity (Gordon, 1991: 19–20, 22–3; Burchell, 1991: 134–40).

The crucial point of Foucault's analysis is that liberalism must conceptualize social order that is compatible with individualism, not only define the proper limits of sovereign power. Foucault argues that civil society is neither a natural fact nor an ideological illusion, but 'the correlate of a political technology of government' (Burchell, 1991: 141). Effective programmes of government provide the conditions of possibility for the social order that make liberal politics coherent. This is most obvious in the thought of the post-war German *Ordoliberalen* for whom the market is not natural. Extensive juridical intervention provides the correct conditions for it as a sphere in which a game of freedom is possible and conduct is perceived as enterprise (1981d: 358–9; Gordon, 1991: 41–2).[13]

Nearly all liberal theory conceals, or is oblivious to, not only the conditions of possibility of society but, along with much other modern political thought, also those of subjectivity. Hobbes's problem is to construct a single sovereign body from a 'multiplicity of individuals'. Yet rather than asking how sovereignty is constituted, Foucault wants 'to discover how it is that subjects are gradually, progressively, really and materially constituted through a multiplicity of organisms, forces, energies, materials, desires, thoughts etc.' (1980e: 97). In so far as sovereignty theory legitimizes power by referring to the willingness of subjects to obey, it is dependent on the practices that have already rendered them obedient (Pasquino, 1986: 99).

No political philosophy is more reliant on the notion of the subject than liberal theory, which assumes that each person exists prior to and independently of society, possessing the faculty to reason without the aid of collective thought. While much liberal theory busied itself with the discursive definition of the abstract, rational, extra-social individual, Foucault highlights the concrete discursive and practical construction of the individual within social institutions. Not only can we not take the liberal individual for granted but there is a vast field, albeit mundane, of an alternative discourse of individuality (as the product of discipline) to be borne in mind (1979a: 194).

Foucault's genealogy can be extended to demonstrate that liberalism is a set of practices for the constitution of subjects. Minson (1985: 145) argues that liberalism transforms the programme of policing in order to produce categories of person, such as youth, elderly, unemployed or single mother. Foucault suggests that neo-liberalism takes the rationale of economic entrepreneurship as a model for both government and a 'widely disseminated conception of individuality as an enterprise, of the person as an entrepreneur of the self' (Gordon, 1987: 300). By regarding all purposively rational conduct as economic, and attributing to subjects the fundamental faculty of choice, self-subjection becomes the key enterprise of the individual producer–consumer (Gordon, 1991: 43–4).[14]

Foucault's analysis of liberalism as a political rationality draws attention to the costs entailed by the forms of government and modes of subjection on which it rests. Only when subjects have been individualized and social cohesion imposed does the liberal problem of 'too much government' make sense. Liberalism's stress on individuality reflects its commitment to the 'individualization' pole of the paradox of humanism. Yet liberal political philosophy obscures the price paid on the 'totalization' side of the account.

The Limits of Foucault's Critics

Contemporary political theorists who criticize Foucault accuse him of incoherence, claiming that his oppositional politics is unjustified, in that it does not rely on reasons for resistance. As Walzer (1989: 191) puts it, Foucault 'calls to resistance – but resistance in the name of what? for the sake of whom? to what end? None of these questions . . . can be satisfactorily answered.' The recognizable reasons are notions of truth, moral values associated with fundamental rights, visions of a better future, and above all, concepts of the human subject. By denying the existence of a human essence or authentic self, Foucault rules out the possibility of an emancipatory politics whose goal it is to liberate the human subject. He contests a whole tradition of Western thought, which considers the inner self to be a realm of freedom, ultimately untouchable by power.[15] This inner self is the core of one's subjectivity, or one's authentic identity. It is also one's autonomous self, in that it is experienced as self-chosen rather than foisted upon one through external, heteronomous pressures. A spatial distinction is established between inner freedom and external danger to that freedom. Foucault subverts this distinction by denying that there is any interiority secure from power which can be emancipated by turning back the forces that confine it. As he departs from the conventional grounds of Western emancipatory politics, it seems to some critics that he denies the possibility of any liberation or gain in freedom.

Truth, values and the subject provide supposedly extra-political foundations for thought, transcending power relations. They are points from which political philosophy can present itself as a sovereign, neutral arbiter which determines the true limits of power. It is held that only with reference to such standards is it possible or legitimate to declare that power has exceeded its limits and must be resisted. However, from Foucault's perspective there are no extra-political grounds on which to stand. Not only is foundationalism a failed philosophical strategy, but it is also one that has costs it conceals. While political power justifies itself in terms of The Human Subject, actual subjects pay the price of humanism.

I shall demonstrate, largely with reference to the arguments of Charles Taylor and Michael Walzer, that when Foucault's critics insist on appeals to extra-political grounds, they exhibit the limits of the discourse of contemporary liberal political philosophy. As they argue about what Foucault may or may not do legitimately, they pronounce the rules that subjects engaging in the discourse must obey. Foucault's critics fall back on the allegedly neutral standards established by their own rules. I argue that the standards they appeal to are neither neutral nor extra-political, but rely on unrecognized and costly political limitations.

Truth as a Limit

Critical humanist political theory, says Taylor (1984: 152, 172), unmasks the domination of power that succeeds only in so far as it disguises itself. He cites a statement by Foucault supporting his view: 'power is tolerable only on condition that it mask a substantial part of itself' (1978b: 86). According to Taylor (174), Foucault must rely on a standard relation 'which makes truth the condition of liberation'. If power masks itself, then there must be a corresponding notion of truth, of what free, liberated, undominated humans would be like. A 'relative gain in freedom' must also be a 'relative gain in truth' for Taylor (1985: 382), the truth referred to being 'our sense of ourselves, of our *identity*, of what we are' (Taylor 1984: 178).

Taylor (1984: 152–3) complains that 'Foucault disconcerts' because he 'seems to repudiate . . . the idea of a liberating truth . . . There is no truth that can be espoused, defended or rescued against systems of power . . . There is no escape from power into freedom.' This is so because Foucault holds that all truth is relative to its particular regime (176). Foucault's relativism renders him 'neutral' or indifferent to changes of regime because 'if all truth is imposition, no change can be a gain' (Taylor, 1985: 383). The new

> regime is identified entirely with its imposed truth. Unmasking can only destabilize it; we cannot bring about a new stable, freer, less mendacious form of it by this route . . . Foucault . . . blocks out . . . the possibility of a change of life form that can be understood as a move towards a greater acceptance of truth (Taylor, 1984: 176–7).

Taylor describes Foucault's position as 'contradictory' (175). The critical force of Foucault's genealogies is lost and redemptive promise erased by his repudiation of liberating truth (152).

Taylor's criticism would be easy to dismiss if he did not recognize, in accord with Foucauldian critique, the limits that are conditions of possibility for the truth he holds.[16] For example, women's suffrage can be justified only in relation to 'who we are', against 'a background of desires, interests, purposes' (Taylor, 1984: 172) with which we have been furnished by 'Western civilization' and which tell us that men and women deserve equal political rights (Taylor, 1985: 382). Because of our humanitarian shared identity which 'is deeply rooted in our more basic, seemingly infrapolitical understandings: of what it is to be an individual, of the person as a being with inner depth – all the features that seem to us to be rock-bottom' (178), we can distinguish significant impositions upon us from trivial influences (172–3).

Taylor admits not only that such solid self-understandings vary between cultures, but that they are internally contested (178). However, his impulse is not to open up the truths we tell about ourselves to political contestation, but to hone down the 'hermeneutically derived understandings of the truth of our self-interpretations' (Taylor, 1985: 383) so that we can arrive at critical judgements about the gains and losses of modernity. Taylor (1984: 164) credits Foucault with bringing to light the often neglected oppressive features of modernity, yet has no doubt that 'we humanitarians' regard something such as the shift from torture to imprisonment as a gain (179). Armed with a true sense of the modern self, Taylor can perform the critical task of philosophy which determines the balance of gains and losses, the latter being excesses of power associated with a 'denial of otherness' (Taylor, 1985: 383). Given that every regime involves some denial, the task is to assess how much, rather than, as Taylor claims Foucault does, regarding all regimes as equally oppressive (378–9).

Taylor's self-interpretation leads him to a single, stable position of judgement because he has already accepted the narrative of progressive humanization that Foucault challenges. For Taylor (1984: 178), 'we cannot shrug ... off' the historical background because it defines humanity for us. Foucault is actually incoherent for Taylor not because of the way the former conceives of power and truth, but because he seems to want to stand nowhere (180).

Taylor forecloses the possibility of judging from the perspective of Western humanism's external and internal contestants. The colonized and marginalized are less likely to consider the spread of modern Western civilization as more gain than loss. They are unlikely to join Taylor in his secure sense of collective identity, his 'we', that enables him to make one judgement for all. Those who resist the totality of his definition of who they are might not regard Taylor's shared understandings as infrapolitical but as political. In spite of his lip-service to diverse points of contestation, Taylor (1985: 384) is interested in tying all of us more firmly to 'who we humanists are' by 'integrat[ing] otherness into more perfect forms of identification'. The effect of Taylor telling the truth about 'who we humanists are' is to determine that those who protest too much are outside the limits of 'our' community, so we need not heed them. His political philosophy of self-interpretive truth may well be able to discern between regimes that offend 'our' deepest sense of who 'we' are and those that affirm it. However, it can do so only by predetermining the limits of the community. It argues from truth but conceals the exclusions that make its truth possible.

However, Taylor (1985: 380) rightly objects to Foucault's generalizations from the regimes of humanist truth to all regimes of truth. He accuses Foucault of obfuscation and rhetoric (382) when he makes statements such as: 'We must conceive of discourse as a violence which we do to things, or, in any case as a practice which we impose on them' (1981a: 68). If all truths are impositions and violence, where is the space for the alternative modes of truth-telling that Foucault favours? Taylor's criticism is helpful when Foucault gravitates to the pole of unbearably heavy truth.

Values as a Limit

Moral value serves as a foundational limit, as the theorist can discern when a regime has offended those values, often embodied in rights, and thus determine the proper limits of power. Walzer (1989: 9) alleges that social 'criticism is always moral in character', challenging practices that do not match up to moral standards. As does Taylor, Walzer avoids explicitly foundationalist positions. He objects to moral argument that is framed by the authority of 'true knowledge' derived from 'God or Reason (or Reason-in-History) or Empirical Reality' (11). He associates attempts to speak in the name of Truth with the posturing of the detached critic (13). In contrast he argues that 'Criticism is most powerful . . . when it gives notice to the complaints of the people or elucidates the values that underlie those complaints' (16). Critics are 'men and women who tell us when state power is corrupted or systematically misused, who cry out that something is rotten, and who reiterate the regulative principles with which we might set things right' (208–9). The moral force of criticism is the application of the regulative principles implicit in a given community.

Foucault's criticism is ineffective as it lacks the principles without which he cannot make the proper distinctions between guilt and innocence (191, 202).[17] Walzer accepts that Foucault distinguishes between the Soviet prison camps known as the Gulag Archipelago and the infiltration of disciplinary power through European society that Foucault refers to as the 'carceral archipelago' (1979a: 298). Rather, his condemnation rests on Foucault's failure to draw a principled moral distinction between authoritarian or

totalitarian and liberal or social-democratic regimes. The principled distinction is that the latter set the proper limits to disciplinary power (Walzer,
1989: 208). Walzer demands from Foucault 'some positive evaluation of the
liberal or social democratic state' (203). For Walzer, one must demonstrate
one's loyalty in order to be a critic (234, 237). Only when critics cleave to
'the constant values of their society' (236) and to common moral references
(230) can they be effective. Having made no oath of fealty to liberalism,
Foucault has no grounds for criticism.

Just as Taylor seems to allow for contending self-understandings, so does
Walzer seem open to multiple directions of social criticism (17). Walzer
appears to accept much of Foucault's argument about normalization (200,
207), but not that the liberal rule of law has itself been compromised by
discipline (207–8). There may be different spheres of justice, but overall
justice is maintained by a discourse that transcends all spheres and defines
the boundaries of the spheres. If law had been normalized, there would
be no reliable embodiment of 'our' supposedly constant morals and values.
If the law operated as a norm, and if by doing so it created delinquents
rather than punishing criminals, Walzer would be unable to draw his
essential moral distinctions between the innocent and the guilty, a distinction he insists not even the guilty challenge (207). He might then be led
to regard this confining distinction as political rather than moral.

Foucault's criticism aims to open up issues such as the guilt or innocence
of prisoners to political struggle (1977i: 227). The law can of course make
its distinctions, which Walzer holds to be moral. The politics Walzer cannot accept is that which challenges guilt and innocence from a perspective
that acknowledges that we are all potentially criminal, and therefore guilty.
Walzer's moral political philosophy, rooted in commonly shared regulative
principles, imposes its own limits by insisting that the distinctions drawn
within liberal regimes, such as between innocence and guilt, are moral
rather than political.

There are, however, textual grounds for Walzer's (1989: 202) sense that
Foucault is neutral about which social system it is better to live under. There
are passages in which Foucault addresses the unbearable heaviness of the
humanist regime, conceiving of liberation projects within it as no more
than rearrangements of modes of subjection. Yet, when Foucault conceives
of alternative arrangements that do not involve the tight bonds between
truth, values and power that characterize humanism, he does appeal to
something he calls ethics. Foucault draws ethical distinctions between
regimes according to the modes of subjectification that they entail.[18]

The Future as a Limit

Walzer (1989: 17) also speaks of the vision of a better future, linked to
sincere hope that it is possible to remedy current ills, as a limit of political

theory. He argues that 'perhaps there is one common mark of the critical enterprise. It is founded in hope ... Criticism is oriented toward the future.' Of course, not all political philosophy need be oriented toward the future, in that much of it aims to justify present orders rather than construct new ones. But to challenge the contemporary arrangements, one must offer a brighter future as 'the role of the critic is to describe what is wrong in ways that suggest a remedy' (10). As Walzer (1985) puts it, only the vision of a promised land provokes people to march out of Egypt and into the wilderness. Not only should the social critic offer us a true interpretation of who we are today, but also 'of what, in our very souls, we would like to be: all our high hopes and ideals of self and society' (Walzer, 1989: 231). Political philosophy oriented to the future discerns between permissible and excessive exercises of power by contrasting future ideals with current reality (233). The contrast motivates people to rectify wrongs and enables them to link local struggles against particular wrongs to a larger vision (239).

Walzer thus alleges that Foucault's critique fails as he has no vision of a better future.[19] Foucault holds that there must always be disciplinary power if society is to cohere, but 'he cannot point to an alternative and better discipline' (204). Foucault 'rattles the bar of the iron cage. But he has no plans or projects for turning the cage into something more like a human home' (209).

Foucault was challenged by arguments similar to Walzer's soon after the publication of The Order of Things, in which he argues that human knowledge does not progress when one episteme replaces another. His critics were worried by the political implications of this argument, which seemed to them to leave no scope for 'progressive political intervention' (1978a: 8). Unlike Walzer (1989: 202), who also equates Foucault's neutrality between epistemes with neutrality between political regimes, these critics held to a foundationalist view of the future. They linked progressive politics to teleology, that is to a conception of history in which the goal or end of history is already given in the underlying principles of the present, such as Reason. Foucault answered his critics by arguing that they constrained progressive politics to a vision of the future which is in some sense 'the same' as the present. In addition, their theories entail a static conception of the future, as a state to be attained which signals the end of history. He was concerned about the possibilities that are excluded by 'a global history of totalities' (1978a: 20). Foucault remarked on the way that politics informed by teleological history legitimizes or condemns revolution depending on whether it is good or bad for the march of History (1981e: 6). Kant could be enthusiastic about the French Revolution as he saw it as a sign of the development of the rational and pacifist moral disposition of the people. It was a step on the way to maturity and to a more humane future (1986b: 90–6). These forms of future-oriented political philosophy determine which acts of resistance are permissible by assessing their contribution to the realization of the goal of history. This approach denigrates the 'immediate' struggles with which Foucault identified his work as they do not anticipate some future liberation (1982a: 211).

Walzer would at first appear not to be restricted by any such singular and narrow visions of the future, as he says that visions should be as plural as are present conceptions of the community. However, we saw above that Walzer forecloses certain perspectives of 'what, in our very souls, we would like to be'. We would not like to be souls who undermine the distinction between guilt and innocence, or who doubt the efficacy of the deployment of principles to regulate the exercise of power. As in Taylor's critique, we would not like to be souls who do not belong to the 'we' which regards progressive humanization as a gain. Walzer's visions of the future are confined to the continuation of this same trajectory, a trajectory which in Foucault's analysis involves its own confinements.

Once again, the criticism levelled against Foucault by Walzer is justified by Foucault's tendency to generalize from his opposition to humanism to human life altogether. Foucault's refusal to discuss reforms or to paint visions of the future should be taken to refer to humanist reforms and visions. Progressive politics aiming toward a humanist future is at cross purposes to an oppositional politics in which we refuse to be who we are, as it urges us to become what we 'truly' are. So long as our hopes and future horizons are defined by the trajectory of humanism, Foucault perceives no rosy picture of the future, and no vision of enhanced individuation that would not also entail increased totalization.

The Subject as Limit

At the most basic level, political philosophy that criticizes excessive power rests on a notion of the human subject. Excessive power is that which represses or encroaches on some or all of the features of the human subject, which as White (1986: 419) says are 'usually developed in terms of concepts such as rationality, intentionality, responsibility, mutuality, interest, etc.' Taylor (1989: 280) derives his conception of who we really are neither from metaphysics nor from natural or human sciences,[20] but from an interpretive 'largely implicit . . . understanding of what the meaning and purposes of human life are'. Moreover, Taylor is willing to agree with Foucault that there is no language that espouses the human grain, meaning some fundamental or essential conception of subjectivity. Our self-understandings remain 'inherently contestable' (280).

Taylor holds that Foucault's concept of power is incoherent. It rests on the conviction that victims are dominated. This requires an understanding of what constitutes significant imposition on those victimized, which can be determined only against the background of shared significance (279–80).

The root of Taylor's difficulty with Foucault is that he stands outside of all shared horizons of significance. If Foucault were not so estranged from this background, he would realise that modern forms of power can empower without simultaneously imposing or victimizing (279). He would be open to the 'civic humanist tradition' according to which 'genuine self-discipline' makes 'possible new kinds of collective action characterized by more egalitarian forms of participation' (Taylor, 1984: 164). In other words, he would see the limits of modern humanist government as more enabling than constraining.

Yet Foucault's is not 'the view from Sirius' (179); it is a view from inside the Western tradition, though the view of those who resist their current subjectivities and therefore do not share the same horizons of significance that Taylor considers rock-bottom. Taylor's position is sustained by his removal of subjectification from the political arena. He claims that it is language, not power, that constitutes subjects (Taylor, 1989: 279). Of course, he says, language constrains us to speak in certain ways at the same time as it enables us to speak, but who would want to be without language? Similarly, in Taylor's view discipline subjects people, but it also empowers them as subjects, so who would want to be undisciplined? Taylor insists that we remain within current horizons of significance by identifying with who we are, which means accepting not only the enabling practices and forces of subjectification, but also the constraining ones. His approach must rule the constraints and limitations that established the boundaries of significance to be off-limits for political contest, because such contest would undermine the solidity of collective identity and might force recognition of those aspects of Western society that are excluded from it. Foucault, in contrast, highlights the costs of current subjectivities and urges us to conceive of ourselves beyond our current limits.

Nonetheless, Taylor's criticism is not entirely off the mark. Foucault does describe modern humanist power as empowerment that is also victimization. Certainly, Taylor (1984: 172) conflates power and domination whereas Foucault does not (1982a: 226), and Taylor constantly refers to power as an imposition. As Connolly (1985: 369) points out, much of Taylor's (1984: 173) case against Foucault rests on his translation of it into his own vocabulary, according to which '"power" . . . is linked with the notion of the imposition on our significant desires/purposes'. Yet Taylor has not misread the general mood of Foucault's opposition to humanism. The interpretive problem arises when Taylor continues to read Foucault as if his project were entirely oppositional, thereby neglecting the affirmative project of potential liberation involved in promoting new forms of subjectivity (1982a: 216).

Foucault's critics delineate some of the constraining parameters of humanist political philosophy by grounding themselves in the limits of truth, value, future and subject.[21] In doing so, they arm themselves with regulative principles that allow them to declare that some exercises of power are excessive while some others are just. These principles are presented as neutral standards of judgement that stand outside political contest, just as the pre-modern sovereign claimed to be above the disputes he adjudicated. However, such philosophical judgements about the proper limits of power conceal and involve other exercises of power. It is as if elaborate philosophical fortresses had been built to repel the enemy of excessive power, but it had been overlooked that some enemies were already within the gates and that the effort to build the walls killed some citizens.

Critics have argued that in the absence of such regulative principles, which would provide him with reasons to resist, Foucault is 'not anarchist so much as nihilist'. The only reason he has for attacking the humanist regime is that it 'is the regime under which he happens to live' (Walzer, 1989: 202). His notion of resistance is deemed to be an irrational 'libidinal response' (Philp, 1983: 46), while his politics are 'irresponsible' because Foucault 'provides us . . . with no way of distinguishing the resistance of the women's movement . . . from, say, the Ku Klux Klan' (White, 1986: 430). These statements, intended to highlight the dangers of abandoning principled critical political philosophy, indicate some of the costs of continuing to adhere to it. Why, as Keenan (1987: 33) wonders, do we need philosophy to draw such distinctions? Does resistance to ethnic cleansing stand or fall with philosophical distinctions?[22]

The cost of relying on such philosophical critiques of power is revealed when confidence in philosophy is lost, perhaps because its extra-political neutrality is no longer credible. Then its advocates feel that the grounds of all political judgement have been undermined. They become nihilists, unable to differentiate between good and bad regimes, between just and unjust policies, or between tyranny and freedom. Foucault's critics rescue themselves from the abyss of nihilism by shoring up their philosophical defences. But what if the excesses of power in the twentieth century have occurred not because the philosophical defences of modern humanism are too weak, but because they are embroiled in those excesses? Should we not then cease asking whether or not to make political judgements without relying on humanist regulative principles, and start working out how to make such judgements? Should we not attempt to think about politics in ways other than those prescribed by humanism? These are the directions in which Foucault's political thought leads.

6

Transgression and Aesthetics

As a discourse which is implicated in the forms of power it aims to limit, humanist political theory cannot promote modes of subjectification that are not simultaneously modes of subjection. It cannot determine the limits that would allow for individualization without simultaneous totalization. The question now is, what could break the snare of the humanist regime? In Foucault's words: 'How can the growth of capabilities be disconnected from the intensification of power relations?' (1984c: 48). Foucault is adamant that it is possible to think in ways other than those defined by humanism, that we can resist, that some form of freedom is attainable, and that new modes of subjectivity can be promoted. His philosophical work is integral to such efforts, as it works against the limits imposed by humanism (44). It

> will not deduce from the form of what we are what it is impossible for us to do and to know, but it will separate out, from the contingency that has made us what we are, the possibility of no longer being, doing or thinking what we are, do or think . . . it is seeking to give new impetus . . . to the undefined work of freedom (46).

Foucault's intellectual, political and ethical project is to go beyond the limits to which humans are subjected (47), taking 'the form of a possible transgression' (45).

Foucault first approaches the theme of transgression in relation to art (1977b). When he returns to the concept two decades later in his central essay, 'What is Enlightenment?' (1984c), he refers to the same issues of the transgression of limits and critical ontology (1977b: 37–8; 1984c: 47). What he means by a critical ontology is an analysis of the limits of our being, not in the sense of an essential, unchanging being but contingent, plural and transformable ways of being human subjects. Critical ontology is conducted as genealogical analysis of the limits to subjectivity which are to be transgressed (1984c: 45–6).

The transgression of limits, as understood by Foucault in his readings of Georges Bataille (1977b) and Maurice Blanchot (1990a), defines the difficult, perhaps literally inconceivable space in which limits are transgressed without being erased. This is the unstable space in which there must always be limits that are both enabling and constraining. 'Transgression is an action which involves the limit.' We only know that there are limits because acts of transgression illustrate their location, revealing how far it is possible to go. 'Transgression forces the limit . . . to find itself in what it excludes.' At the same time, transgression is relative to the limit it violates: 'to what void does it owe the unrestrained fullness of its being, if not that which it crosses in its violent act and which . . . it crosses out in the line it effaces?' Thus transgression is not the opposite of the limit, but the illumination of limits, 'like a flash of lightning in the night which . . . owes to the dark the stark clarity of its manifestation'. Transgression is not 'a victory over limits', but a form of 'nonpositive affirmation', like Blanchot's 'contestation' according to which one proceeds 'until one reaches the empty core where being achieves its limit and where the limit defines being'. Transgression does not overcome limits, restore the repressed and instigate the rule of freedom, but shows that what we are, our being, depends on the existence of limits. To overcome limits would be to end being, which is necessarily finite (1977b: 33–8).

Transgression is more than the analysis of limits, as it demonstrates that no limits are absolute. The most absolute limit was embodied in the existence of God, who revealed Man's finitude while proclaiming his own infinity and positively affirming a limitless being exterior to the realm of limits. God was a 'word that surpasses all words', designating something more than could be expressed in any language. The death of God 'discloses . . . the limitless reign of the Limit' by denying the possibility of an existence beyond limits and non-positively affirming the limited nature of all being (30–2). The possibility of transgression depends on recognition of the limitedness of the limit. Yet it is not easy to experience transgression because in the contemporary world the spheres of transgression, in particular sexuality or eroticism, have been absorbed by anthropological (or humanist) discourses. They confine transgression to unilluminating reversals of prohibitions (30, 50). So Foucault turns to particular, self-reflective forms of art, literature and philosophy that make transgressive moves by revealing the limits of language and thought without attempting to exist beyond them.

Transgression, then, is not only difficult to conceive but is inherently unstable. There are only acts and moments of transgression, rather than firm grounds and secure sites. Foucault often associates transgression with awareness of and proximity to a void or an absence. Transgression is a risky act of teetering on the edge of an abyss into which one might fall. Foucault does on occasion fall into this void, when he suggests the possibility of thinking, living or creating without limits. He is tempted to leap into the abyss of unbearably light being as if freedom were a safe place beyond all limits. The space of transgression as work on limits is the precarious and uncertain space between the two poles of unbearable lightness and unbearable heaviness, of absolute unlimitedness and complete limitation. This is the proper space for Foucault's transgressive thought. However, just as Foucault is drawn in his condemnation of humanism to portray all human existence as unbearably constrained, so does he tend to depict its alternatives as unbearably light. This chapter traces Foucault's moves between unbearable lightness and transgression in the spheres of art and the relation to oneself as a work of art.

Transgressive Art

Modernist art is often associated by Foucault with transgression of limits. Foucault relates to avant-garde literature as both a site of freedom and as critical perspective, in both cases its power being derived from its self-referentiality and reflexivity. It 'has freed itself from the necessity of "expression"; it only refers to itself' (1977e: 116). This is not only a question of a self-conscious relationship with other paintings and texts (1977d: 92), but of a 'self-reflexive pursuit of the origin of language [which] leads to the repeated discovery of the lack of foundation of language, the "essential void" at its center' (Carroll, 1987: 115). Modernist literature and art comes as close as possible to the void by concerning itself with the absence of a foundation of discourse or of representation.[1] Avant-garde art and the works of the mad philosophers are associated with experiences such as madness that transgress cultural limits (1965: 278).

There is a temptation to conceive of the non-space of literary transgression as a secure site of freedom. Although 'the language in which transgression will find its space and the illumination of its being lies almost entirely in the future', there is a hint that it exists at least partially in the present (1977b: 33). 'We must try to assimilate . . . these extreme forms of language in which Bataille, Blanchot, and Klossowski have made their home' so that they might 'serve as the basis for finally liberating our language' (38–9). A new language, he hopes, will arise from the absence of the philosophical subject at whose inner core the 'mad philosopher' can find 'the transgression of his philosophical being' (41, 44). Foucault at points privileges literature as if it were a site of freedom, outside the modern episteme (1973b: 43–4). Elsewhere Foucault seems to want to recapture the voice of madness and to reanimate its 'primitive force of revelation', according to which one day the reality of the world will be reabsorbed into madness in a 'delirium of pure destruction' (1972b: 38–40; trans. Carroll,

1987: 112). From a critique of the limits of ourselves as sane beings, Foucault jumps to insane negativity.

According to Carroll (1987: 129), Foucault's work 'fluctuate[s] between a negative but nonetheless transcendent aestheticism – and a disruptive, critical paraesthetics', meaning a critique that draws on aesthetics for its transgressive force.[2] Carroll sees Foucault wavering between an aesthetic unbearable lightness and critical work on limits, thus identifying the source of the tension in Foucault's work between the poles of heaviness and lightness in his writing on art. This insight explains why, in his later work, Foucault turns to aesthetics of the self as a form of transgression.

Foucault's predominant view of transgressive literature is that it reaches the limits of what can be said, without attaining the untrammelled freedom of saying it. Bataille tries to speak of the unconscious and taboo, but language fails him (1977b: 39–40). Similarly, despite his nostalgia for the transgression of madness, Foucault denies that 'mad' art can succeed in speaking madness where rational discourse fails. The works of Nietzsche, Van Gogh and Artaud express a consciousness of absence and silencing of madness, not madness itself (1972b: 39–40). Madness, in this light, is not a position of freedom, beyond the constraints of rational discourse, but illuminates the limit of Man. That is why neither Nietzsche nor Van Gogh could produce paintings or philosophy in a state of madness. Madness, like death itself, is in the void beyond transgression. Transgressive art takes us right up to the void, exposing what is absent. 'It is the world that becomes culpable . . . in relation to the work of art' and that 'must justify itself before madness.' It is forced to recognize that there is something beyond itself of which it does not have the measure, which it does not control, such as madness (1965: 287–9). The 'mad' philosophers and poets evoke the experience of madness in that they teeter on its edge, indicate the limits of discourse and celebrate the presence of absence, refusing to avoid the void.

In his treatment of modernist literature Foucault on the whole avoids the danger of identifying freedom with disruptive force and regarding art as naturally autonomous. Literary transgression is not a transcendence of limits, but a recognition of finitude.[3] Modernist literature 'gives prominence . . . to the fundamental forms of finitude'. Extending language to its limits leaves Man 'not at the very heart of himself but at the brink of that which limits him' (1973b: 383). Revelation and definition of finitude does not enable humans to escape it. Transgression is not a site beyond limits, but consists in work on them.

Aesthetic Relation to Oneself

The ethical turn in Foucault's work can be understood as his attempt to transgress the limits of humanism through 'a critique of and an alternative to modern self-subjugation' (Bernauer, 1990: 9). According to Deleuze (1988: 96), after the impasse of *History of Sexuality* (1978b) whereby attempts at liberation reinforce repression, Foucault sought a third axis in addition to power and knowledge as a way for us to get free of ourselves. This third axis is the ethical relation to oneself, whose corresponding mode of subjectification is an aesthetics of the self, which has recourse neither to knowledge nor to universal rules. Given that there is no essential subject, 'that the self is not given to us, . . . there is only one practical consequence: we have to create ourselves as a work of art' (1984b: 351). One relates to oneself as an object of art which one must create. One's life becomes the material for aesthetic activity, the aim being to give it a certain beauty.

Aesthetics of existence is a mode of ethical self-formation. Foucault approves of Baudelaire's ethos of modernity as a model of an art of the self, understanding it as 'a mode of relationship that has to be established with oneself', involving 'the asceticism of the dandy who makes of his body, his behavior, his feelings and passions, his very existence, a work of art . . . Modernity . . . compels him to face the task of producing himself.' Two features of this ethos are worth noting. Firstly, it is 'a discipline more despotic than the most terrible religions'. It may be autonomous, but it is no free-for-all. Secondly, 'this ascetic elaboration of the self' cannot occur in society or the polity, but only in 'a different place, which Baudelaire calls art' (1984c: 41–2). More so than we, Baudelaire lived in a time when there was no room in political thought for an asceticism of the self (1988p: 14). One way to understand an aesthetics of existence is as a stylization of conduct, or more simply as a lifestyle (1987b: 92–3).

Most of Foucault's work on aesthetics of the self focuses on the Classical Greek and Hellenist eras. The Greeks offered Foucault the fascinating idea of life as material for a work of art (1984b: 348), while we share with antiquity 'the search for new styles of existence as different from each other as possible' (1988r: 253). Foucault endorses the formal or conceptual conditions of the Greek and Hellenist relation of self to self; i.e. the loosening of the connections between the three axes of subjectification: power, truth and ethics (Deleuze, 1988: 100). The possibility of freedom lies in loosening the tight stranglehold of the triadic relation within which we are subjected. Foucault insists that 'we have to get rid of this idea of an analytical or necessary link between ethics and other social or economic or political structures' which was linked to a fear 'that we couldn't change anything, for instance, in our sex life or our family life, without ruining our economy, our democracy' (1984b: 350). We must detach our ethical relations with ourselves from the government of others, while also understanding that 'it's not at all necessary to relate ethical problems to scientific knowledge' (349). Aesthetics of existence also corresponds to an 'absence of morality', in the sense of obedience to a universal code of rules (1988q: 49). The Greeks and Hellenists indicate alternative forms of individualization focused on the aesthetic construction rather than on a scientific and moral discovery of the self.

In the Greek era, the 'ethical substance' consisted of pleasures that were liable to excess, to be untimely, or inappropriate to ones's social status (1987b: 54–60). The mode of subjection took the form of self-mastery in the face of pleasures to be moderated following a 'principle of stylization of conduct for those who wished to give their existence the most beautiful and accomplished form possible' (1987b: 250–1). This is an aesthetic relation to one's life, to oneself (1984b: 341), involving 'intentional and voluntary actions by which men not only set themselves rules of conduct, but also seek to transform themselves'. As such, Greek ethics were neither universal nor did they require knowledge of the truth about oneself. They indicate attempts 'to make . . . life into an oeuvre that carries certain aesthetic values' in contrast to our psycho-technologies of the self (1987b: 10–11).

While Greek ascetics are detached from scientific definitions of the self, unlike modern subjectifications, they are not uninvolved in political relations, as the regulation of others was associated with mastery of the self. Their techniques of the self, associated with dietetics (the health of the body), economics (the husband's running of a household) and erotics (men's love of boys), took the form of combat with pleasures to be mastered. They were of the same nature as techniques for the government of households and of cities (1987b: 65–72). Moderation understood as control of pleasures entailed freedom from oneself and thereby a domination of oneself, as a condition for domination over others. Modes of government of the self and of others were isomorphous (1987b: 76, 83), as they are in the modern era of state pastoralism.

Foucault claims that ethical self-formation became a more reflexive operation in the Hellenist era (1984b: 348). The care of the self involved certain exercises that could be differentiated from the practice of virtue itself. These exercises were techniques of 'ethics/knowledge'. There were testing procedures to check what one was capable of and what privations could be borne. There was self-evaluation, an inspection of one's day in which one considered how errors could be corrected. A more constant exercise was needed to screen representations in order to prevent attachment to what was not under one's control (1988o: 58–64). Self-mastery remained the telos of Hellenistic ethics but took the form of a self-possession, enabling one to enjoy oneself for one's qualities independent of one's political position. It was the self-mastery of a rational being in complex, reciprocal relations rather than simple domination (1984b: 357–8).[4]

Foucault argues that as self-formation became increasingly oriented towards knowledge, it also aligned itself more closely with universal rational rules. The personal choices of aesthetics gave way to the universal obligations of all rational beings in late Stoicism (1984b: 356). The problem of giving one's life correct form was still relevant, but this became 'a universal form . . . grounded in both nature and reason, and valid for all human beings (1988o: 238). The art of living grew more conformist and constraining, though relations of domination were replaced by greater reciprocity.[5]

Foucault does not prefer Greek non-universal, non-scientific aesthetic ethics of domination over Hellenist ethics. Although an isomorphism between ethics, economics and politics remained, the model of government for which one trained was far more reciprocal than before, in marriage as well as politics (1988o: 80). Conjugal fidelity was no longer the expression of an ideal self-mastery, but a recognition of one's essential, natural, rational being (184). One's behaviour must accord with a universal form, a form which connects individuals to each other in relations of dependence and independence. This ethics is a far cry from one suitable to a world in which the ethical subject was always master (238). After the classical Greek era Foucault looked forward to a 'time when the art of the self would assume its own shape, distinct from the ethical conduct that was its objective'. Then techniques of the self 'would begin to have an independent status, or at least a partial and relative autonomy' (1987b: 77). Even if later Hellenist ethics were more constrained by knowledge of the subject,[6] they detached the relation with oneself from domination of others.[7]

Foucault objects to the connection in classical ethics between attention to the self and domination of others (1988k: 19). He finds nothing either exemplary or admirable about the Greek stylization of conduct, which never made itself available to all but remained an elite practice (1988r: 244). He condemns the social conditions of possibility for such aesthetics, i.e. a 'virile society with slaves, in which women were underdogs'. Relations involved 'dissymmetry, exclusion of the other, an obsession with penetration . . . All that is quite disgusting!' (1984b: 344, 346).

Foucault does not value self-formation in itself, without considering the socio-political context in which it is conducted. Nothing in contemporary culture would seem closer to the care of the self than 'the Californian cult of the self', according to which

> one is supposed to discover one's true self, to separate it from that which might obscure or alienate it, to decipher its truth thanks to psychological or psychoanalytic science, which is supposed to be able to tell you what your true self is (1984b: 362).

Foucault insists that this is another reprehensible attempt to discover the essential subject, and thus diametrically opposed to an aesthetics of the self. His aesthetics of the self or stylization of life cannot be translated into the contemporary parlance of 'lifestyles'. These lifestyles rely on scientific and pseudo-scientific notions of the self proposed by 'experts'. They are also chosen (and often exchanged) from a range of options determined by the

market, which is perhaps the most effective form of constraining government in the contemporary West. Foucault was hesitant to claim that a
notion such as 'the care of the self' could become 'the center of a new
philosophical thought, of another kind of politics' (1988p: 13). He was
interested only in an ethics or stylization of life which is not shackled to
political power and scientific truth.

In Foucault's eyes, classical ethics also offers a degree of freedom by
'bypassing Christianity' (1988r: 249). For Foucault, Christian modes of
subjectification were almost synonymous with self-renunciation (1984b:
366), mortification (1981f: 239) or refusal of the self (1993: 215).[8] Christian
subjectification introduced the notion of a self with a deep interiority that
could be known only through constant self-examination (1985a: 24–5).
Morality was made dependent not only on self-knowledge, but also on a
theory of the subject (1988r: 253). Each soul was thought to be in danger of
being seduced by evil thoughts, which can only be exposed through verbal
confession (1993: 219–20). Evil was identified in Christian ethics as willfulness and attachment to oneself or Satan (220). Complete obedience
to one's spiritual superior was required to preclude such willfulness (216).
In Christianity, the responsibility for caring was removed from oneself to the
spiritual guide or confessor, who relied on an intimate, individualizing
knowledge of each soul in the flock (1981f: 236–7). Christian ethics
established 'a link between total obedience, knowledge of oneself, and
confession to someone else' (239). Confession was itself 'renunciation' of
oneself, a 'self-sacrifice' that 'finds its parallel in the model of martyrdom'
(1993: 220–1). Indeed, during the first centuries of Christianity its techniques
of the self were less confessional than penitentiary, involving physical acts
of ritual martyrdom (1988j: 43).[9]

Foucault's understanding of Christianity bears close resemblances to his
notion of humanism. Both entail tight bonds between truth, power and
morality. Modern humanist power is conceived as pastoral power, which
was an originally Hebrew concept, but one preserved and modified by
Christianity (1981f: 240). Confession, the telling of truth about oneself, is
the main technique of power operating in the deployment of sexuality
(1978b: 58), as it lies at the centre of 'the strange and complex relationships
[that] developed in our [Western] societies between individuality, discourse,
truth, and coercion' (1993: 201). Modern subjectivity has been tied to the
truths it tells about itself, or its hermeneutics of the self, which begin with
Christianity (204). The cost of Christian truth about oneself is that

> the revelation of truth about oneself cannot be dissociated
> from the obligation to renounce oneself . . . you will become the
> subject of the manifestation of truth when and only when you
> disappear or you destroy yourself as a real body or as a real
> existence (221).

Modern humanist Western culture has replaced the Christian self-sacrificial hermeneutics of the subject with a positive philosophy and practice of subjectivity (222). Both enhance the individual at the cost of increasing constraint, totalizing power as they individualize the subject. Both demand the sacrifice of human subjects.

Foucault's Aesthetics

Foucault affirms an aesthetics of existence and care of the self, uncovered only by going back to the Greeks, as transgression of the limits of Western Christian-humanist culture. In order to clarify this strategy, it should be determined whether Foucault has a notion of a beautiful subjectivity which we should strive to fashion for ourselves, and what are the formal features of the aesthetics he has in mind.

In his aesthetics of existence, Foucault does not direct us to a certain subjectivity or a preferred identity. What is relevant to Foucauldian aesthetics of the self is not any particular beautiful subject but the process of subjectification as an art. Greenblatt (1980), whom Foucault cites as one of the few studies of aesthetics of existence done since Burckhardt (1987b: 11),[10] argues that the freedom of arts of the self consists not in self-creation itself but in the experience of self-formation in the face of all the other forces that fashion us. It is an irony of self-fashioning that despite its resonance of autonomy, it includes being moulded by outside forces and attempting to fashion others. There is an interaction of control mechanisms that belies any belief that one is entirely what one made oneself, though Greenblatt (1980: 257) feels the need to sustain the illusion that he is the principal maker of his identity: 'To abandon self-fashioning is to abandon the craving for freedom, and to let go of one's stubborn hold upon self-hood, even selfhood conceived as a fiction, is to die.' So, Foucault may admire the dandy for his self-fashioning as a rebel, but above all he admires him for recognizing 'first and foremost the burning need to create for oneself a personal originality' (Baudelaire, 1964: 27). Foucault finds in Baudelaire a model of self-invention and production that is undertaken in spite of the predominance of subjection in the contemporary world.

There are three central features to Foucault's aesthetics of the self: the demands of style; artistic practice as a source of empowerment; and work with present conditions and limits. Both Foucault and Nietzsche admire the Greeks and Romans for introducing style into life as well as art (Nehamas, 1985: 39).[11] According to Nietzsche, what matters in the construction of oneself is the imposition of a single style or taste, entailing a self-mastery in which one manages to integrate all one's traits into a coherent individuality. The general principle is that arts of the self are a stylization of conduct by means of practices of the self. The lesson to be learnt from the artists is that creation of form is not a matter of spontaneity, impulsiveness, licentious abandonment and irrepressible energy. Rather, their secret is that they know that the feeling of freedom and creative capacity is greatest when acting of necessity (Nehamas, 1985: 195). To style oneself 'involves controlled multiplicity and resolved conflict' (7). Foucault also discusses practices of the self as *askesis* (1987b: 72–7), in its Greek sense of self-discipline rather than a Christian sense of self-denial (1988o: 43).

Foucault's aesthetics of existence designates artistic practices and techniques of self-empowerment. These techniques

> permit individuals to effect by their own means or with the help of others a certain number of operations on their own bodies and souls, thoughts, conduct, and way of being, so as to transform themselves in order to attain a certain state of happiness, purity, wisdom perfection, or immortality (1988j: 18).

Foucault does not maintain that all such techniques of the self escape embroilment with techniques of domination, but they are potentially forms of power that enable. It is through artistic, creative activity that we experience ourselves as agents with power. Here also Foucault follows Nietzsche, for whom artistic activity exemplifies agency, thereby enabling us to experience autonomy and to enact our will to power (Warren, 1988: 179, 141, 139). The need to experience self-formation is a demand to realize the full promise of humanism which it cannot fulfil because it is trapped in the double of totalization and individualization.

Foucault's aesthetics of existence works on the limits of the present. The empowerment developed through stylization of oneself is needed to withstand the oppressive constraints of the present. This agonistic relation with the present is evident in Baudelaire's aesthetic. Dandyism achieves its special mode of relating to the present as the apparently idle observer of the city and crowd. The present is understood by Baudelaire (1964: 13) as 'the ephemeral, the fugitive, the contingent, the half of art whose other half is the eternal and the immutable'. Close attention to the beauty of the age rather than an abstract and unobtainable invariable beauty is exemplified by the portrayal of contemporary costume. For Baudelaire, concern with the transitory, with the clothed body, constituted a willingness to extract beauty from corrupted sinful life in contrast to futile attempts to capture a soul untainted by original sin (Moers, 1960: 79–81). In Foucault's mind, this attitude is an ironic heroization of the present. Baudelaire's aesthetic of working with corrupt materials rather than conceiving the ideal is

> a desperate eagerness to imagine [the present], to imagine it otherwise than it is, and to transform it not by destroying it but by grasping it in what it is. Baudelairean modernity is an exercise in which extreme attention to what is real is confronted with the

practice of a liberty that simultaneously respects this reality and violates it (1984c: 41).

Close attention to reality is critique; its violation is transgression. Yet even transgression is never 'beyond' the present. Whatever new modes of subjectification may be devised will be crafted from the corrupted materials of our present selves.

Foucault's work on the limits of current selves indicates that Foucault does not return to a notion of an immutable or essential subject that is always endowed with the capacities to transform itself. When there is resistance, it is because of the capacity of 'already existing categories of persons' (Wickham, 1986: 159), whose subjectivity is also a function of the degree of domination, equality or reciprocity they have with other subjects. If we do have liberty, that is because the power relations that constitute us and exist between us as subjects also empower us. Depending on the balance between enabling limits and constraining limitations, between lightness and heaviness, we have more or less capacity to create ourselves as works of art. Arts of the self are themselves intended to enhance individual capacities without also increasing the power of subjecting government. Far from aiming to eradicate all manifestations of subjectivity, Foucault promotes new forms of subjectivity that evade the self-renunciation and sacrifice entailed by Christian-humanist culture. He does not 'return to the subject', but resignifies subjectivity.[12]

Aesthetic Autonomy

Foucault suggests that by engaging in aesthetics of existence, human subjects have the capacity to disentangle the interlacement of ethics, truth and power and thus to attain a greater degree of liberty. Foucault does not explain why he turns to aesthetics in order to become free, leaving the impression that he makes a familiar appeal to art as a privileged realm of freedom in Western culture. According to this line of reasoning, when in the modern West art lost its previous religious function, it became a purposive activity that had no visible purpose. The attainment of beauty serves no social function, being pursued for its own sake. Art is not constrained by the demands of technological functionality, scientific veracity or moral validity. Art can thus be defined as autonomous or autotelic, in that it gives itself its own laws and ends.[13]

It might seem that self-referential, autotelic art has nothing to do with politics. However, the realm of art is also regarded by critics of modernity as a sort of refuge for all those aspects of human life and culture that have been forgotten, excluded or repressed by Western modernity. The complaint is that the West has become increasingly disenchanted, to use Weber's phrase, as it becomes progressively rationalized, or ordered according to the demands of rationality. Feelings, emotions, imagination, bodily sensation, especially the extremes of desire and eroticism, and even madness, are all displaced. Such critique has been endemic to the West since the rationalist Enlightenment, which provoked the Romantic movement. It is considered legitimate as long as it keeps to its proper limits, safeguarding the integrity of this aesthetic or expressive sphere of culture. However, it is not legitimate to assert aesthetic standards in the realms of instrumental and substantive rationality or to attempt to detach the expressive sphere from the others and withdraw into it.[14]

Several critics argue that Foucault adopts an illegitimate, aestheticist posture, taking artistic transgression to be a site of freedom that transcends all limits. According to Rajchman (1985: 16–17), until 1977 Foucault put his faith in the transgressive force of avant-garde literature which expresses all that is excluded by ordinary discourse. Megill (1985: 2) locates Foucault within a Romantic tradition that tends to see 'art' as the primary realm of human experience and the world as an aesthetic phenomenon created by humans as artists. While the expression of loss is acceptable, aestheticism is bound to be defeated by reality. Moreover, Foucault's support for the new social movements of marginal groups such as women, gays and radical ecologists is said to rest on 'an aesthetic subject' which highlights those aspects of subjectivity excluded by modernity, i.e. 'pre-rational embodied otherness', as well as 'spontaneity and expressiveness' (White, 1986: 422–4). If this were so, then Foucault as a political theorist would be as foundationalist as his critics, because he would be appealing to extrapolitical grounds in order to determine the proper limits of power. He would in effect be arguing that power must not violate the creative and expressive capacities of humanity. Foucault would be aiming for untrammelled freedom that transcends all limits.

Critiques that present Foucault as predominantly aestheticist and unbearably light are one-sided, overlooking the specific features of Foucault's (and Nietzsche's) aesthetics. Yet they have a certain credence because Foucault does not critically analyse his appeal to aesthetics. According to Foucault, three axes (truth, power and ethics) constitute the formal limits of subjectification. Aesthetics is not included in the picture. Rather, it seems to have the capacity to detach ethics from power and truth. As Flynn (1988: 115) notes, Foucault would have to address the place that art and the discourse of aesthetics has in modern Western culture in order to analyse its limits. He would also have to make some effort to determine what the practical and political conditions of possibility for universalized aesthetics of existence would be.

Foucault's relative inattention to the conditions for aesthetics of existence is evident in his brief remarks about the background conditions of Greek and Hellenist ethics. As Foucault realizes, there are social and political constraints on members of the elite who supposedly make free, personal choices (1988p: 11). Their care of the self is deeply implicated in complex relations with their peers, polity and society (7). Foucault's desire to un-hinge the 'analytical . . . link between ethics and other social or economic or political structures' (1984b: 350) should be carefully qualified. One may attempt to conceive of an art or care of the self in non-scientific and non-juridical terms, but transgressive work on limits must take into account current constraints. In order to sustain the transgressive intent of arts of the self, it must be shown that they are deeply involved in political processes. If they were not, Foucault's turn to care of the self would be politically uninteresting. Foucault confuses the conceptual differentiation of aesthetic ethical self-formation from power, truth and morality, with an actual or practical detachment of the axes of his genealogies. The basis of this confusion is his lack of analysis of the enmeshment of art in power relations. The realm of art is not one of unbearable lightness, although Foucault's transgressive moves sometimes indicate that it is. The following two chapters examine Foucault's theoretical and practical transgressions, including the temptations to escape all limits.

7
Theoretical Transgression of Limits

Foucault's analysis of the limits of humanism suggests that they are unbearably heavy. In contrast, there are moments at which Foucault responds to the overwhelming limitations of humanism with unconstrained abandon. At others, he suggests that there are privileged sites of transgressive thought and action that guarantee possibilities of resistance in all regimes. The richness of Foucault's work lies in the tension between these two poles of heaviness and lightness. Thus, although Foucault adopts contradictory positions, my intention is not to establish which are most appropriate to the essence of his work, but to illustrate how his thought is constituted in the space between the two poles. This chapter will examine how, in spite of the temptation to lightness, Foucault's unstable positions on issues of power, resistance, subjectivity, truth, knowledge, thought and aesthetics of existence oscillate between lightness and heaviness. I also argue that Foucault's transgressive middle course in relation to power and resistance implies regulative principles for the assessment of regimes, alluding to an ethic of permanent resistance.

Power and Resistance

The issues addressed in this section are: what makes resistance possible, what constrains it, and what prevents power from being unbearably heavy? This requires further elaboration of Foucault's notion of positive power. Power and resistance are conditions of possibility for each other. While Foucault asserts that 'power is co-extensive with the social body; there are no primal spaces of liberty', he also insists that 'there are no relations of power without resistances'. In other words: 'To say that one can never be "outside" power does not mean that one is trapped' (1980h: 141–2). Foucault does not consider power to be evil, and hence does not anticipate a society without power (1988p: 18–19). There are two angles to

Foucault's position here. Firstly, all subjectifying power endows subjects with some capacities required to be agents, even when it is oppressive. Moreover, there are techniques of the self which are exercises of power, intended to bring about positive effects on oneself (1988j: 18–19). As power in a positive sense enables subjects, one could not and would not wish to exist outside its limits.

Secondly, Foucault understands power relations to be the 'means by which individuals try to conduct, to determine the behavior of others' (1988p: 18). Relationships of power permeate the whole social body and all human relations (3), and, given Foucault's concept of techniques of the self, must also exist within individual subjects. Power is defined as 'a mode of action upon the actions of others' (1982a: 221). Since each society is a complex, ongoing structure governing the way some actions act upon other actions, it would be nonsensical to conceive of a society without power (222–3).[1] In other words, any society limits the ways in which some actions limit other actions. A society without such limits is not a society just as a subject without limits is not a subject.

For Foucault a world without power would be unbearably light. However, Foucault's conceptualization of power suggests that resistance is unbearably light, in that it is always possible. If it is always possible, it is unlimited. Foucault states that 'there cannot be relations of power unless the subjects are free' (1988p: 12). All power relations which are attempts to direct the conduct of others can be conceived as 'strategic games between liberties' (19). The recalcitrant actions of free subjects resisting attempts to direct their conduct are a necessary condition for the exercise of power. Power cannot be a physical determination, and thus 'slavery is not a power relationship when man is in chains' (1982a: 221). Foucault distinguishes his concept of power from states of domination which might conceivably be so complete that 'the way one determines the behaviour of others is so well determined in advance, that there is nothing left to do' (1988p: 20). Domination is, in Foucault's view, a special case of power relations, widely prevalent in the modern era, which have consolidated or locked together in 'a massive and universalizing form' (1982a: 226).

Foucault's definitions make it possible for him to state that: 'Where there is power, there is resistance' (1978b: 95). But the corollary is that where there is domination, there is no resistance. Given that modern regimes constitute domination, in the form of carceral, disciplinary society and bio-power, Foucault's terminology would induce a sense of entrapment. As Baudrillard (1980) and Dews (1987: 188) suggest, in his substantive historical works Foucault tends to depict the operations of power from the perspective of the programmes of the power/knowledge regimes, such as Bentham's panoptical scheme, which he analyses. Foucault is thus induced to overestimate their success in normalizing the whole social body (McNay, 1992: 39).

However, Foucault does not mean to claim that resistance is impossible in modern humanist regimes. He remains confident that resistance is possible because power relations do not solidify into states of complete domination. Having viewed how power arises from below in its micro-physical forms (1978b: 94), composed of different tactics and heterogeneous techniques, Foucault suggests that 'power is in reality an open, more-or-less coordinated (in the event, no doubt, ill coordinated) cluster of relations' (1980k: 199). There is 'no doubt' because power relations are always fragmented, competing with each other and operating in different sites along different lines (1978b: 94–5).

Foucault's optimistic assertions about the possibility of resistance are unconvincing in comparison with his portrayals of domination, because he pays insufficient attention to the fragmentation and inconsistencies of contemporary modes of government and subjection. For example, he argues that imprisonment fails as a strategy to reform inmates, but he does not explain how prisoners are able to resist their subjection. In Foucault's presentation, the juridical values of the law are completely overwhelmed by scientific-administrative norms. Yet prisoners appeal to the rule of law when they resist because its uncomfortable articulation with normalizing disciplines constitutes what Foucault would call an 'odd term in the relations of power', one of the knots at which resistance occurs (1978b: 96).

Foucault also fails to elaborate much on the capacities for resistance with which we are endowed by humanist subjection. According to his 'rule of the tactical polyvalence of discourses' (1978b: 100), a discourse of power can be reversed into one of resistance. For example, the discourses that constructed homosexuality as a subspecies enabled homosexuals to claim their rights as a natural minority (101).[2] The basic argument is that gays are not responsible for their sexual orientation which cannot therefore be considered a moral offence. So any discrimination against them is unjust. However, Foucault does not generalize from these suggestions as he could. What, for example, is the potential of a democratic or popular surveillance of government that he mentions in some lectures? (Gordon, 1991: 24–7). Democracy institutes reversals of the direction of the panoptical gaze. In general, all forces of individualization, although matched by forces of totalization, can be deployed at points of weakness in the humanist regime.

The possibility of resistance can thus be explained in terms of the ill-coordination of power relations and capacities for resistance which subjects have. However, Foucault does not make these arguments clearly, so that resistance is drastically undertheorized in his work. As a consequence, humanist regimes are portrayed as more coordinated than they are, while the many ways in which they enable subjects to resist are overlooked. Foucault's overall assessment of humanism is thus one-sided, as Taylor (1984: 164) and others complain.

Without theorizing resistance, Foucault's own formulations about what makes resistance possible are opaque and allude to some sort of underlying, indomitable essence of agonal subjectivity that always resists power. Such resistance would be unconditioned and thus unbearably light. One possible source of an indomitable essence is the body, which Foucault hints at in his unelaborated suggestion that the attack on bio-power should rally around 'bodies and pleasures' (1978b: 157). The frequency with which Foucault designates the body as the target of power (1979a: 26; 1978b: 151–2) lends credence to the critical view that Foucault presupposes that the body is an essential subject. Although Foucault emphatically denies that Man can understand himself as a body, because the 'body [is] totally imprinted by history' (1984a: 83), this itself suggests that there is something solid which is printed upon (Butler, 1989: 602–3). Foucault is tempted to regard the body as a site of transgression and the source of revolt. Yet his wider project is to disrupt the appeal to any untouchable, deep interiority whether it is located in the human body or soul. When Foucault writes that 'the soul is the prison of the body' (1979a: 30), he indicates that the disciplining of the body occurs as much through its psychological as its physical effects. So neither the soul nor the body can be privileged as sites of freedom or the grounds of revolt.

Foucault also states that:

> there is indeed always something in the social body, in classes, groups and individuals themselves which in some sense escapes relations of power, something which is by no means ... primal matter, but rather an inverse energy ... a certain plebeian quality (1980h:138).

Yet this 'plebs ... is not a real sociological entity ... There is ... no such thing as "the" plebs' (137–8). He suggests that exercises of power always provoke their own resistances, defining the plebs 'as not so much what stands outside power relations as their limit, their underside, their counter-stroke, that which responds to every advance of power by a movement of disengagement' (138). Each power relation seeks to extend itself to the point where it 'can direct, in a fairly constant manner and with reasonable certainty, the conduct of others' (1982a: 225). As it does so, it generates an adversary reaction on the part of those others, whose resistances are not only 'a reaction or rebound ... doomed to perpetual defeat' (1978b: 96), but themselves strive to become the winning strategy (1982a: 226).[3] Foucault claims that when relations of power congeal into hegemonies they are apt to provoke consolidated resistance in the form of revolutions (1978b: 96).

Resistance is possible when power pushes towards its limits. Power relations should always be analysed in terms of adversarial struggle and confrontational strategies. There must always be points of insubordination at which it is possible not to escape power *per se*, but to escape the particular strategy of power relation that directs one's conduct. Each adversarial relation is potentially reversible (1982a: 225–6). The term that best characterizes Foucault's concept of adversarial, strategic, potentially reversible power relations is 'agonism' (222). The word suggests a contest involving strategy, reaction and even taunting, as in a wrestling match.[4] Agonism may be as serious as political domination or as light as child's play. It permeates all the different types of relationships (economic, familial, communicative and sexual) within which power relations are immanent (1978b: 94).

There is, however, one sense in which resistance becomes absolute for Foucault. All regimes and structures of power reach their limit when people give 'preference to the risk of death over the certainty of having to obey', which is 'that moment when life will no longer barter itself, when the powers can no longer do anything, and when, before the gallows and the machine guns, men revolt'. No power can continue to rule over people who refuse to be intimidated by death (1981e: 5). Foucault discusses here the Iranian revolution,[5] about which he was accused of being unduly enthusiastic, but he refers to the Warsaw ghetto revolt as involving the same degree of intensity and defiance.[6] When a regime becomes merely destructive, it ceases to govern (1982a: 220). An act of suicide would demonstrate the limits of a power relation (1988p: 12). Certainly in the context of bio-power, 'death is power's limit, the moment that escapes it' (1978b: 138).

Foucault is too enthusiastic about revolt that demands the ultimate sacrifice.[7] His admiration for the spiritual, revolutionary experience as a way of life suggests a mode of living that transcends the limits of normal life. Yet he is simultaneously aware that such existence is sustained by a momentary light that will soon die out (1988f: 218–9). Absolute transgression is a lightning flash, not daylight. Less dramatic but more continuous acts of resistance may be more significant affirmations of agonistic liberty (Thiele, 1990: 922–3). Another objection is that if bio-power has made this the century of genocide, how will the willingness to die limit the oppressive power of regimes that do not wish to govern whole populations but to murder them? Death and sacrifice may indicate the limits of power but they are not its insurmountable impasses. As in Tian An Men Square, sometimes when governments order the tanks to crush the bodies in their path the soldiers obey. Foucault's enthusiasm for revolt that costs lives is unbearably light because while life may be lived as resistance, death cannot be lived. It is a transgression that escapes all limits.

With these qualifications in mind, Foucault's argument that revolt as refusal to obey demonstrates the limits to power remains valid. To some extent, all political power is conditional upon the cooperation and obedience of its subjects, who always have the potential to withdraw their consent and thus defeat tyrannies (Sharp, 1985: 151). Foucault argues that such revolt stands in the way of 'absolute absolutism' and anchors all forms of liberty (1981e: 5). It is not the existence of universal rules and doctrines of natural rights that limit power, but practices of liberty (5, 8). 'Liberty is a *practice* ... [I]t is never assured by the institutions and laws that are intended to guarantee [it]' (1984g: 245). Liberty should not be considered as a secure state of liberation unbreached by excesses of power, but as the practices that effectively limit power (1988p: 2–3). It is not the philosophical critique of power that limits its excesses, but practical critique in the form of resistance.

Ethic of Permanent Resistance

Political theorists critical of Foucault argue that he fails to provide motivation or reason to resist, which is a necessary condition for revolt. In contrast, Foucault implies that no such philosophical motivations or justifications are necessary. Those who are engaged in refusal are 'all those on whom power is exercised to their detriment, all who find it intolerable' (1977h: 216). This feeling is common to a series of struggles that have developed since 1968, including the feminist movement, campaigns against parents' power over children, the medicalization of social problems, anti-psychiatry and general opposition to the administration of daily lives (1982a: 211–12). What matters is frustration with and resentment of the present, including ourselves, rather than a better alternative (Hoy, 1986a: 14).

Foucault does not answer the question: 'Is there or is there not a reason to revolt? Let's leave the question open' (1981e: 8). However, Foucault's conceptualization of power relations as agonistic implicitly includes a regulative principle for the assessment of political regimes. If there is legitimation for resistance in Foucault's work, it is that it is the condition of possibility for further resistance and the constitution of agonal subjectivity (Thiele, 1990: 918). A regime is judged unfavourably as dominative because it minimizes the possibilities for strategic reversal and thereby confines practices of liberty (1988p: 3). The regulative aim should be to pursue 'games of power . . . played with a minimum of domination' (18). The question to be asked is 'whether the system of constraints in which a society functions leaves individuals the liberty to transform the system' (1983b: 16). Is the system open to agonistic struggle? Nurturance and affirmation of agonism thus sustain the active, participatory capacities of subjects required for both resisting domination and the establishment of alternative regimes.

Foucault consistently refuses to close off the options that resistance might make available. Foucault proclaims 'that to imagine another system is to extend our participation in the present system' (1977i: 230). The intellectual is likely to find that his programme becomes an instrument for repression

(1988i: 10). It seems to be inevitable that the effort to conceive of a totally different politics fails, that the 'new order' always adopts something of the old in order to function. There is no guarantee that the state of affairs brought about by resistance will be better than the present, as any social arrangement or definition of community may become oppressive even if it is instituted by acts of resistance against a previous regime. Yet we would not be doomed to resign ourselves to the consequences of excessive or misdirected resistance: the future is not forever. Each new arrangement instituted by revolt may itself be resisted.

Foucault's positions on liberty as practice and agonistic openness lead his politics to what I refer to as an ethic of permanent resistance. Foucault comes closest to defining this ethic when he says:

> The ethico-political choice we have to make every day is to deter-mine which is the main danger . . . My point is not that everything is bad, but that everything is dangerous . . . If everything is dangerous, then we always have something to do. So my position leads not to apathy but to a hyper- and pessimistic activism (1984b: 343).

The incessant activism that such vigilance calls for is the engagement of agonal subjects who seek not the end of struggle, but the liberty of participating in it. They forego the hope and comfort that there is some safe haven external to power relations, as this vision is no more than a mirage. Pessimistic inaction overwhelms subjects who have been striving to reach the mirage, only to discover that there is no oasis of eternal respite. For Foucault, ethics is 'the practice of liberty' (1988p: 4), entailing perpetual transgression of limits. Our fight is our freedom, our struggle is our art, and our resistance is our existence. This is not a cry of despair, but an affirmation of life as it is. An ethic of permanent resistance is an approach to life which is at once playful and serious; both unbearably light and unbearably heavy.

Truth and Thought at the Limit

Resistance, permanent or sporadic, includes some thought, as thought 'always animates everyday behavior' (1988h: 155). In the analysis of the unbearable heaviness of humanism, thought and knowledge seem to be extremely constrained by the limitations of epistemes and regimes of power/knowledge. How, then, can those who resist free themselves from humanist thought or understand the constraints of humanist government? As Foucault claims to offer such knowledge and critical thought, how can he justify such claims? If all knowledge is enmeshed with power, in which power/knowledge regime is Foucault's work entangled? What is the status of Foucault's work when his arguments about power/knowledge are referred back to his archaeologies and genealogies? These are not insurmountable philosophical difficulties for Foucault's work, but he sometimes hints that his work is unconstrained by limits when he is tempted toward the unbearable lightness of truth and thought.

Foucault holds that his archaeological and genealogical critique can 'separate out from the contingency that has made us what we are, the possibility of no longer being, doing, or thinking what we are, do, or think' (1984c: 45–6). Critical analysis of limits uncovers the limitations of one's thought and life, enabling one to overcome the constraints. It is a critique of how we are subjected in relation to truth, rules and ethics, all of which are events of thought. Philosophy as understood in classical times, as 'an exercise on oneself in the activity of thought . . . enables one to get free of oneself . . . [T]he effort to think one's own history can free thought from what it silently thinks, and so enable it to think differently' (1987b: 8–9). New historical conjunctures give rise to new ways of conceiving issues such as madness or sexuality, as well as new solutions for them. One examines how the different solutions to a problem have been constructed, while analysing how these solutions are the result of a particular form of problematization. So, Foucault's historical critique demonstrates that the possibility of thinking differently is contingent on changing conditions (1984f: 388–90). Thought is transgressive work on limits when it is construed within the limits of present thought. What one can do is to expose the unchallenged assumptions implicit in our practices and thought (1988h: 154).

Yet Foucault is tempted to conceive of thought itself as unlimited freedom. 'Thought is freedom in relation to what one does, the motion by which one detaches oneself from it . . . the study of thought is the analysis of freedom' (1984f: 388). Philosophy seems to be reinstated as a privileged discourse: 'all the work that has been done to think otherwise, to do something else, to become other than what one is – that, too, is philosophy' (1988g: 330). The very *raison d'être* and ethics of an intellectual are 'to make oneself permanently capable of detaching oneself from oneself' while 'altering one's own thought and that of others' (1988s: 263–4). It seems that freedom can be achieved and constraints escaped with ease and without transgressive practice.

Foucault's temptation towards unbearably light thought can be traced back to his early work, where he encounters literature that explores language's absent foundation. The humanist tradition generally locates free thought in deep subjective interiority. In contrast, Foucault argues that what he calls 'the thought from the outside' lies where 'the speaking subject disappears' (1990a: 13–16). He finds in Blanchot's writing a language that expresses a 'pure exteriority' that 'nothing can limit' (11) because it floats in a foundationless 'infinite void that opens beneath the feet of the person it attracts' (28). Yet, in this explicit discussion of attraction to the pole of limitless existence or absolute transgression, Foucault argues that language, not speaking subjects, can exist without limits. Language is limitless because it does not originate with the meaning supposedly given it by the human subject. The 'pure outside' is a philosophical space which is outside the foundations of humanist subjectivity, like the death of philosophical Man envisaged at the end of *The Order of Things* (1973b: 387). Concrete, living subjects remain tied to all the non-philosophical constraints.

Thought is properly transgressive only when it is practical as well as philosophical (1984c: 45). Greek and Hellenist philosophies, such as Stoicism, Epicureanism and Cynicism, are practices of the self and modes of stylization of one's life. Foucault proposes to revive this approach of living as well as thinking philosophy as an ethos.

> The critical ontology of ourselves has to be considered as an attitude, an ethos, a philosophical life in which the critique of what we are is at one and the same time the historical analysis of the limits that are imposed on us and an experiment with the possibility of going beyond them (1984c: 50).

We know what we are (our ontology) only by understanding the limits that make us what we are by defining our form. Limits are revealed by the lightning flash of transgression through the effort to go beyond them, an effort which paradoxically can reinforce the limit (1990a: 34–5). The knowledge of ourselves that Foucault supposes is available to us is not really an ontology. Work on our limits transforms us by altering some of the present limits and instituting new limits. Knowledge of ourselves is thus as transitory as the transgressive flash that illuminates limits.

The knowledge that Foucault's work offers is transitory, experimental and unstable, but is not immune to the attractions of the limitless freedom of a pure outside. In Foucault's archaeological work, he claims that:

> In every culture, between the use of what one might call the ordering codes and reflections upon order itself, there is the pure experience of order and of its mode of being (1973b: xxi).

The Order of Things was written as the analysis of this experience, as if there were a transcendent position from which Foucault could perceive the limits of cognitive orderings of the world. Without doing more than extensive archival research, Foucault appears to attain a state of critical reflection at which a culture 'frees itself sufficiently to discover that these orders are perhaps not the only possible ones or the best ones' (1973b: xx). Such reflection occurs in a *heterotopia* where the very grounds of any categorization are destroyed (xv). On the one hand these *heterotopias* are identified by means of works of art (Don Quixote, Las Meninas, Sade) that illustrate the breaks between epistemes.[8] The return of foundationless language in general heralds the end of the modern humanist episteme (382–6), while a certain kind of literature seems to have remained autonomous of the episteme all along, keeping alive the experience of madness or the being of language (1965: 31). On the other hand, Foucault ascribes his detached thought to an austere empiricism that makes possible a *'pure description of discursive events'* which is visible from 'that outside in which . . . enunciative events are distributed' (1972a: 27, 121).

Both aesthetic and empiricist pure exteriority are untenable forms of transgressive thought, detached from practical work on limits. There is no space in which one can speak intelligibly that is not subject to the limits of an episteme or discursive formation. It is precisely the limits, or the rules of discourse, that make statements meaningful. Foucault recognizes the invalidity of speaking from a position of pure exteriority: 'It would not behove me, of all people, to claim that my discourse is independent of conditions and rules of which I am very largely unaware' (1973b: xiv). We are not reliable analysers of our own archive (1972a: 130). We can never think 'above and beyond' what we already are as we never know ourselves outside of all the conditions that both constrain us and endow us with our subjectivity as thinking beings. In this light, Foucault's *heterotopias* are not non-spaces beyond all systems of ordering but places of uncertainty at the limits of one episteme and the beginnings of another. Archaeology places itself in thresholds that indicate the fragility and contingency of any episteme (Carroll, 1987: 62). It suggests that orders different from those which we consider natural are possible by going to the margins rather than stepping outside epistemes. Just as resistance is possible because of the ill-coordination of techniques of power, so is the archaeological perspective possible at points where epistemes conflict.

Transgressive knowledge is as unstable as the points of disarticulation of discourse at which it becomes possible. However, Foucault is tempted to unbearably light knowledge when he adopts apparently fixed positions for his critique. Genealogy is defined as 'the union of erudite knowledge and local memories which allows us to establish a historical notion of struggles' (1980e: 83). The erudite knowledge is Foucault's archival work, which reveals how the apparent coherence of human scientific knowledge conceals the struggles by which such coherence was established (81–2). The other side of genealogy is 'local, discontinuous, disqualified, illegitimate knowledges' (83). Some are not systematic enough to be considered science, some are customary, and some are disallowed because their enunciators, such as psychiatric patients, are not supposed to know much about themselves (82). Together, erudite and local knowledge constitute an *'insurrection of subjugated knowledges'* (81). They are 'anti-sciences' in that they struggle against 'the effects of the power of a discourse that is considered to be scientific' (83–4). Genealogy is 'effective history' understood as the 'affirmation of knowledge as perspective' (1984a: 90). The perspective affirmed is that of those who resist.

Foucault's account of the union becomes problematic when intellectual work is subordinated. Although theory 'is an activity conducted alongside those who struggle for power . . . aimed at revealing and undermining power where it is most invisible and insidious' (1977h: 208), intellectuals do not contribute to the awareness of 'the masses' who resist. The latter have full knowledge of the power they oppose, so the task left to intellectuals is to unblock the channels for the articulation of the masses' subjugated knowledge by acting as relays (207). But do the oppressed have such easy access to a privileged 'counter-discourse' (209)? Spivak (1988) criticizes Foucault and Deleuze for overlooking the enormous difficulty the heterogeneous groups who constitute 'the masses' have in understanding the systems that oppress them.

The wisdom of the oppressed that Foucault is sometimes seduced by is not truly transgressive but is always limited by its reverse relation to that which it opposes as the flip-side of the coin. Foucault himself (1980f: 130) was unhappy with the way the struggle around the prisons developed as an isolated campaign of ex-prisoners and social workers. 'It has allowed itself to be penetrated by a whole naive, archaic ideology which makes the criminal at once into the innocent victim and the pure rebel.' Such romanticism, with its 'lyrical little chant' was not 'valid political currency' because it simply identified with one group of oppressed without taking account of their place in wider political networks.[9] Seduction to the easy, light knowledge of the oppressed occurs in the absence of critical analysis of the conditions of possibility of their knowledge.

Foucault's critical considerations of the discourse of the oppressed show that 'there is not, on the one side, a discourse of power, and opposite it, another discourse that runs counter to it' (1978b: 101). What makes a discourse useful for resistance is not simply its derivation from the mouths of the oppressed, as they can either turn around a dominating discourse (e.g. the demand for recognition of the 'naturalness' of homosexuality) or find that their discourse has been appropriated by the dominant social forces (e.g. the commercialization of punk). To determine the utility of discourses for resistance we must assess at what point of a power confrontation they *are* used (102).

'Specific' intellectuals, i.e. professionals operating in their local area of competence, can help others precisely because they are vested with a certain responsibility and power on the basis of their close association with true discourses (as their producer, consumer or distributor) (1980f: 126–33). Because they are complicit in power relations, specific intellectuals can be effective critics. An analysis that links the production of the truth about criminals to a wider network of social sciences and techniques of government might be less dramatic than a lyrical chant, but it suggests the grounds for an alliance of struggles. Such 'theories' act as relays by linking the perspectives of 'specific' intellectuals, tracing a general picture of how power works on the basis of positions in it. These positions must always be assessed in terms of their adequacy to struggles against subjection, not in terms of their advocacy of oppressed subjectivities such as delinquency.

Foucault's work is criticized for having an unbearably light attitude towards the necessary limits of truth as embodied by the demands of epistemology, which establishes the proper standards for truth. Foucault states that:

> I have never written anything but fictions . . . It seems to me that the possibility exists for fiction to function in truth, for a fictional discourse to induce effects of truth, and for bringing it about that true discourse engenders or 'manufactures' something that does not as yet exist (1980j: 193).

Megill (1985: 235–45) understands from this that Foucault means that the world is all text and therefore can be remade by rhetoric. Foucault admits that he tells lies that can bring about change because the world itself is limited and constituted only by discourse. Megill adopts a realist position according to which there is a real world out there whose effects we feel directly, like being hit by a truck, without the mediation of any cognitive interpretation (42, 53, 83, 101–2). From a realist perspective the question asked of any knowledge is always how accurately it reflects reality. So we would ask of Foucault how faithful his analyses of humanist subjections are to a fixed reality.

Megill's realist approach illustrates one of the ways in which political theory is assessed according to its epistemological validity. As several commentators have noted, Foucault brackets out this epistemological concern (Fraser, 1981: 275; Paden, 1987; Schneck, 1987: 15–16), giving the impression that he is neutral about whether human sciences are actually true. From his argument about the mutual constitution and enmeshment of power and knowledge it follows that efforts to justify theories epistemologically cannot be disentangled from their political effects. However, he does not mean that because all human scientific truth is enmeshed with power relations, both in determining what counts as true and in the circulation of knowledge, it is untrue (1988p: 17). To do so would be to follow the logic of humanist epistemology, according to which true knowledge must not be contaminated by power.

Foucault, however, is not *politically* neutral about the truth of the human sciences as he is concerned with their effects. While Foucault's critique undermines noble, untarnished transcendental notions of Truth, he raises no radical objections even to the truths of the 'dubious' human sciences, associated with domination, that he analyses (Gutting, 1989: 273, 276). Foucault does not deny the therapeutic effectiveness of psychiatry (1988p: 16). Similarly, an account of the conditions of possibility of modern medicine is not an attack upon its ability to cure (1973a: xix). The reason that 'genealogies . . . are . . . anti-sciences . . . is not that they are concerned to deny knowledge . . . it is really against the effects of the power of a discourse that is considered to be scientific that the genealogy must wage its struggle' (1980e: 83–4). It is the wider effects of sciences such as psychiatry, criminology and psychoanalysis in terms of government and subjection that Foucault objects to, not the sciences themselves.

The issue for Foucault's 'anti-sciences' is whether, given the current limitations on true discourses in contemporary regimes of power/knowledge, Foucault's writing can push us beyond those limits. Do Foucault's genealogies, as reinterpretations of our past, disrupt the lineages of current identities and open up scope for new ones? Can we tell, not lies, but different truths about ourselves that will become 'true' if aesthetic practices of the self succeed? Foucault's writings are, as Deleuze, suggests, tools (cited in 1977h: 208). The limit on them is the demand that they prove useful.

Foucault avoids the trap of permanently privileging the knowledge of his archaeologies and genealogies above other knowledge. If he did, he would represent the truth of his work as unbearably light, unconstrained by conditions of possibility. Foucault's writings do not express the enduring truth. He wants them to serve 'as an instrument, a tactic' and to be like 'Molotov cocktails', but also 'like fireworks, to be carbonized after use' (1985b: 14). The fictions about ourselves and the world that might become true are not irrevocable states of freedom, but contestable, contingent and transitory positions. Moreover, as we can never fully know our limits or fully go beyond them, the critical analysis of limits is never done. '[T]he theoretical and practical experience that we have of our limits and of the possibility of moving beyond them is always limited and determined; thus we are always in the position of beginning again' (1984c: 47). Parallel to an ethic of permanent resistance is an ethic of perpetual rewriting of the truth of our limits. The truth, like the future, is never forever.

Foucault's attitude towards truth is also not unbearably light in the sense of dismissing its value. Indeed, he insists that the 'task of telling the truth is an endless labor' (1988s: 267). However, he resists the constraint of telling only scientific truths, disrupting the tight bond between truth and science in our political economy of truth (1980f: 131) by telling non-scientific truths. 'I believe too much in truth not to suppose that there are different truths and different ways of speaking the truth' (1988q: 51). He focuses on the Greek notion of truth-telling as *parrhesia* to elaborate a form of political truth that can be spoken to resist governments.

Parrhesia is the practice of speaking one's mind, often in situations in which it is dangerous to do so because of the power of one's interlocutor.

This role of frank criticism, taken as a duty, is played by someone who speaks out against the majority in a democracy or against a monarch (1983d: 2–8). *Parrhesia* is credited with enough moral force to limit political power (13), providing that the *parrhesiast* practises a care of the self that harmonizes his words with his deeds (63). Some forms of *parrhesia* focused on the personal sphere, improving the lives of individuals, while others were politically oriented to the betterment of the state (68). Foucault recovers in the tradition of *parrhesia* an alternative to the epistemological focus on *how* we know that what is said is true. The alternative is to consider the moral and political *effects* of telling the truth (4, 114).

At the time of his research into the seemingly obscure texts about *parrhesia*, Foucault was engaged in *parrhesiastic* criticism of the French government's policy of non-intervention in Poland around the Solidarity movement and Jaruzelski's coup, based on the grounds that it was an internal affair (1983e; 1988s: 267). Foucault claimed that the government's position was both untrue and immoral, arguing that the inaction of previous governments in face of the overthrow of progressive regimes in Spain in 1936 and Hungary in 1956 had been immoral, as tyranny went unopposed, and had international consequences beyond each state's 'internal' sovereignty (Eribon, 1991: 299).

Foucault proposes that there is a role for truth-telling in today's politics. Indeed, there is no way to challenge dominative regimes of truth other than to criticize politics on the basis of some form of truth. The domination of one game of truth can be escaped only by beating it at its own game, as with the truth told by the ecology movement, or playing another game of truth, such as Foucault's genealogies (1988p: 15). The prospect of a game of truth 'without constraint and without coercive effects' is utopian (18), as truth always has its limits. However, as in the field of power and possibilities for resistance and self-fashioning, the aim must be for games of truth to be played with a minimum of domination (18). The question in both spheres is not whether all limits can be transcended, as that would make being and truth unbearably light; nor is it to determine necessary and eternal limits that can never be transgressed, which would make for unbearable heaviness; rather, the question is how limits can be constructed that sustain and affirm agonistic openness. This returns us to the practice of transgressive work on the limits of ourselves and our present, and in particular to Foucault's transgressive work on himself.

8
Practical Transgression of Limits

The first section of this chapter examines Foucault's own transgressive practices: intellectual writing, gay culture, and sadomasochism. Each practice is assessed as transgressive work on limits, while their problematic tendencies towards unbearable lightness are presented as dangers. The ramifications of Foucault's attitude to gay culture for identity politics are also discussed. In the second section of the chapter, I dispute claims that Foucault's practices of and concern for the self constitute a withdrawal from politics. As transgressive work on limits is both intellectual and practical, arts of the self are also political arts, reinventing subjects who are always located within networks of power, thus requiring resistance to existing modes of subjectification and government.

Transgressive Practices

Foucault demands of contemporary intellectuals an ethic of self-detachment which is not one of academic abstraction, but an 'elaboration of self by self' (1988s: 264). Painstaking self-transformation demands periodic alterations of one's intellectual positions (1988l: 14). Intellectual self-transformation is not achieved by mere reflection, but through writing. Foucault noted how writing was used in Greek and Hellenist arts of the self within practices of self-regulation (e.g. 1984b: 363–4). He was also fascinated by the avant-garde writer Roussel, in part because of his 'attempt at modifying one's way of being through the act of writing', to the extent that 'the subject who is writing is part of the work' of a writer (1987a: 182, 184). Foucault describes his theoretical work as 'fragments of an autobiography' prompted by his unsettling experiences with other people and institutions (1988h: 156). He consistently constitutes himself as a personality through his writing.

Writing, however, can tempt one toward absolute transgression, as when

Foucault states: 'I am no doubt not the only one who writes in order to have no face' (1972a: 17). It is one thing to transform oneself, when 'one writes to become someone other than who one is' (1987a: 182), but quite another to totally dissolve oneself. James Miller (1993: 147) suggests that Foucault was influenced by Roussel, who pursued the limits of language to expose the void at the heart of its function as signifier. He did so at the cost of much personal anguish, involving insanity and drug use (1987a: 164–7), leading to his death, and perhaps suicide, by overdose (J. Miller, 1993: 33). Yet Foucault was attracted as much to Roussel's language games that revealed the finitude of the meaning-giving subject, as to the pursuit of limits that risked unbearable lightness by approaching death (1987a: 176).

Many of Foucault's other practices of the self induce attempts to transgress all limits, as they are unconstrained in their total opposition to humanism. He talks of 'the destruction of the subject as a pseudosovereign' by means of 'the suppression of taboos and the limitations and divisions imposed upon the sexes; the setting up of communes; the loosening of inhibitions with regard to drugs' (1977i: 222). Drugs have the potential to enable one to think in ways other than one's habits of thought, by unifying and differentiating experiences in unusual ways (1977f: 190–1). Foucault embraces 'all those experiences which have been rejected by our civilization or which it accepts only within literature' (1977i: 222). Moreover, 'it is possible that the rough outline of a future society is supplied by the recent experiences with drugs, sex, communes, other forms of consciousness, and other forms of individuality' (231). A vision of the future is given as the opposite or reversal of the present.

When transgression takes the form of simply violating the law and trespassing taboos, however, it is no guarantee of liberty and is likely to reinforce power. One would expect Foucault to be more wary of the conditions under which contemporary drug cultures, for example, are the focus of campaigns of social hygiene and law enforcement that intensify oppressive techniques of power. Given Foucault's disdain for the Californian cult of the self (1984b: 362), he might have asked how liberating new forms of consciousness really are, considering that New Ageism has become yet another lifestyle option. Rock music is also identified by Foucault as a cultural form which constitutes a 'way of life', fashioning attitudes and responses beyond musical taste (1988n: 316). Yet it is also a key means of seducing youth into the circulation of cultural commodities in the market. All these experiences have transgressive potential, but as there are no privileged or secure sites of resistance, their effects must be assessed carefully.

Gay Lifestyle and Identity Politics

Above all other forms of practical transgression, the lifestyle of particular concern to Foucault was being, or rather becoming, gay. The lifestyle he conceives is one of resistance to bio-power and normalization. Cohen (1988: 89) notes how little acknowledgement of Foucault's gay identity there is in current scholarship, although Foucault does not have a static notion of identity. 'One should not be a homosexual, but one who clings passionately to the idea of being gay' (quoted in Kritzman, 1988: xxiii). As Cohen (1988: 93) suggests, Foucault's conception of an aesthetics of existence may well be drawn from his understanding of the transgressive potential of becoming gay. Foucault refused his subjection as a homosexual. He resisted being bound to an identity that was defined in the nineteenth century according to a supposedly sexual nature (1978b: 42–4). He does not deny his sexual orientation, but rejects the limitations imposed by a science of sexuality that treats it as an ineluctable fact of nature. 'What the gay movement needs now is much more the art of life than a science' (1984h: 27). What is crucial is the conscious choice to be gay and to live one's life differently, as no behaviour patterns can be deduced from the category of 'homosexual'. There is not a homosexual nature which possesses determined attributes. The task is

> to advance into a homosexual *askesis* that would make us work on ourselves and invent . . . a manner of being that is still improbable . . . To be 'gay', I think, is to try to define and develop a way of life . . . [that] can yield a culture and an ethics (1989d: 206–7).

The promise of the gay community and culture lies in its invention of ways of relating (1982b). Love, affection, tenderness and intimacy between men have not been tolerated (1989d: 205). While close friendships between women including physical contact have been put up with, only in prisons and armies have men been allowed to be friends (208–9). 'The development towards which the problem of homosexuality tends is the one of friendship' (204). Foucault does not deny that same-sex relations and sexual pleasure would be at the core of the envisaged lifestyles of friendship. However, the wider significance of gay friendship is the proliferation of new forms of relations between people beyond those currently sanctioned, namely marriage and the family. One of the present's unbearably constraining features for Foucault is the poverty of institutionally permitted relations. '[H]omosexual culture . . . is . . . the instruments for polymorphic, varied and individually modulated relationships' (1989d: 209). By inventing new relations, it promotes new forms of subjectivity.

Foucault's conception of becoming gay, as a sexuality that is created rather than discovered in oneself, has ramifications for gay (and other) identity politics. The standard argument is that gay politics is based on a natural sexual identity, thereby establishing a commonality of interests which can be articulated by representatives and fought for in the political arena. Foucault does not denigrate the value and effectivity of seizing scientific discourses of sexuality and turning them against those who use them to exclude marginal groups. Both homosexuals and women have been able to use the sexual natures constructed for them as the basis for the demand that they be recognized as different but natural (1977k: 155). However, Foucault was not interested in reversals that simply affirmed what had been repressed, be it sex, madness or delinquency, but in those that begin with such affirmations in order to dissolve the categorizations or subjections that construct sexual or other natures (159). So he recognized the importance of struggling for rights to sexual freedom, but only as a stage, or as a condition of possibility for the affirmation not of identity but creativity (1984h: 27).[1]

Foucault holds that identity politics has its unbearably high costs. Identities are fashioned by political technologies of individuals which totalize as they individualize. On the basis of such identities we recognize ourselves as members of a social group or state (1988k: 146). The same political logic according to which a gay man identifies himself politically as a member of the gay community induces citizens to lay down their lives in defence of their states. When identity is taken to be natural in relation to a larger social or political entity then, as Rajchman (1991: 103) says, we are confronted by the identities of nationalism or racism. Not only are people tied to identities that are designed to be governable, but they are prepared to participate in mass sacrifice of themselves and others in wars to defend their identities. Perhaps gays will not be convinced to sacrifice themselves or others for the sake of their 'race'. Yet they were identified by the Nazis as a source of degeneracy and thus a threat to the race (1978b: 118–19). Now they are blamed for the AIDS plague, another threat to the race (Bersani, 1988: 201–4). It is dangerous to be tied to identity, especially a 'natural' one.

Collective identities also exact costs as the grounds for normalization. Foucault argues that 'if identity becomes *the* problem of sexual existence . . . people . . . will turn back to a kind of ethics very close to the old heterosexual virility' (1984h: 28). Foucault holds that gay culture resists normalization, but is aware that the abnormal can establish its own normality. This is partly because social acceptance is sought by becoming normal, restricting gayness to a private affair of sexual preference while portraying gays as another minority whose rights have been violated (Bersani, 1988: 205–6). Normalization also occurs because the gay community is entangled in networks of power relations. The lifestyle promoted in gay culture for uncloseted, middle-class whites may be remarkably like straight consumer lifestyles, aiming for 'liberation through accumulation'. As Cohen (1991) argues, the affirmation of distinct difference by a group entails the suppression of difference within that group. If 'we' are all gay in the same way, then those who experience different desires and pleasures must not be 'us'.

Foucault's interest, in contrast, is in 'relationships of differentiation, . . . of innovation . . . not ones of identity' (1984h: 28). The multiplication of relations and pleasures is an ethic of permanent resistance to normalization.

Advocates of identity politics argue that despite the costs, collective action must be grounded in secure identity. Foucault argues that a critical political community can only be a temporary group organized around similar concerns (1984f: 385). For Foucault, what constitutes the gay community is its critical challenge to the poverty of present affective relationships and pleasures. Transgressive work on gay identity proceeds by using the capacities of the sexual self to create new pleasures (1984h: 28).

Sadomasochism

Foucault chose to pursue his pleasures and ethic of anti-normalization through practices that have been considered abnormal and perverse even by other gays, as well as heterosexuals. True to his philosophical ethos of living as well as thinking at the limits, Foucault practised S/M (sadomasochism), for a short period in France, then enthusiastically after being introduced to the scene in San Francisco (J. Miller, 1993: 90–1, 259–62).[2] S/M has been labelled dangerous, an obstacle to the social acceptance of gays, as well as politically incorrect because of its fascination with domination and submission (Thompson, 1991: xi–xii). Often, sado-masochists have been excluded from the gay and especially lesbian community because they offend its sense of identity.[3] On a much broader scale, humanist culture is repulsed by sadomasochism. S/M remains one of our taboos, testing the power of our sympathetic imagination (J. Miller, 1993: 377).

The relation between transgressive practice and S/M has been discussed by Miller (1993: 87), who identifies the connection between Bataille's interest in sadomasochistic eroticism as a form of transgression and Foucault's adoption of it as a 'limit-experience'. Limit experiences consist of experimental practices on the self which tear the subject from itself in an attempt 'to reach that point of life which lies as close as possible to the impossibility of living' (1989b: 31). These are, then, the same as transgressive practices that work on limits while teetering at the edge of the void of unbearable lightness.

Foucault believes that S/M is a transgressive limit experience because of its 'eroticization of power, the eroticization of strategic relations . . . *the use* of a strategic relationship as a source of pleasure' (1984h: 29–30). S/M is a practice of liberty that plays with power, involving theatrical, ritualistic scenes in which one or more participants take on the dominant role and the partner or partners the submissive role.[4] However, in S/M this is literally a game, and the relation supposedly 'is always fluid' because the 'roles can be reversed' (1984h: 29; Samois, 1987: 36). While non-practitioners tend to focus on the issue of pain, the central theme for practitioners is generally power (Samois, 1987: 7–8, 16, 64). The eroticized relationship is combative (185), like the struggles of agonal subjects.

Agonal subjects delight in the liberty of struggle rather than seeking a world without power. Some practitioners of S/M share Foucault's concept of power, arguing that playing with power is itself empowering (Thompson, 1991: xviii, 7). 'Power is not evil. Power is strategic games' (1988p: 18). Experience of power in the self, of positive capacity and energy, or of a 'coming to power', is by no means limited to the dominant players in S/M (Samois, 1987: 38, 43, 95, 183–4). Power relations in S/M are not quite what they seem: power has to be negotiated before a scene is begun, during which the submissive exercises the power to incite the dominator and of enduring pain (189–90).

Critics of S/M argue that it replicates oppressive, patriarchal, misogynist and misanthropic power relations in its cruel theatre of (self)-hatred (Linden et. al., 1982: 4, 176). Put starkly, they claim that in patriarchal society all relations, especially sexual ones, are sadomasochistic, positioning men as sadists and women as masochists.[5] In contrast, its practitioners argue that they deal explicitly with the issues of power, trust and victimization that make up any relationship but which are often unrecognized (Thompson, 1991: 182). The ideal of a relationship based on an equal share of power conceals inevitable power relations and tensions which constitute a relationship (28, 32). The occlusion of power relations has its costs.

S/M is also the key to Foucault's strategy of 'desexualization', meaning the invention of 'a general economy of pleasure not based on sexual norms' (1980j: 191). The assault on the citadel of bio-power requires radical tools. It begins by converting what is scientifically defined as sexual perversion into the invention of new pleasures, utilizing the unruliness of desires that might be denounced but cannot quite be governed, like the unruly 'plebs'. The aim is 'to push personal and public boundaries on the sexual frontier as far as they will go' (Thompson, 1991: xvi). The feelings induced by S/M are described as 'out-of-mind-and-body experiences' (Thompson, 1991: xix). S/M succeeds as a transgressive practice in so far as it dissipates the boundaries of the body within which identity is supposed to reside. The differentiations of domination and submission, pain and pleasure, mind and body, inside and outside, are undermined and blurred in S/M. Ecstatic erotic practices all lead to 'little deaths', or the death of the subject as a consolidated unit (1977b: 31–3, 40). The deep interiority of the self is, while the experience lasts, dissolved as the external, bodily or somatic boundaries of the self are transgressed.

Yet the transgressive moments attained through S/M are precisely that – moments, or flashes. As ecstatic moments they may be bearable, at least to some, but one cannot live a life of such moments. Foucault's attraction to the ecstasies of S/M is to a large extent an attraction to unbearable lightness and an urge to transcend subjectivity altogether. The psychic construction of the S/M scene combined with intense, extreme physical sensation is said to produce a 'transcendental experience' and 'altered states of consciousness' (Thompson, 1991: 224, 171–2). In ecstatic moments the self is shattered but not refashioned.

The validity of S/M as a transgressive practice of the self is also cast into doubt because it can be reintegrated into dominant modes of power. Foucault suggests that San Francisco's S/M ghetto was coopted by the pleasure industry (1984h: 28). The claims of practitioners that they can completely transcend pervasive power relations through theatrical ritual is untenable (Linden et. al., 1982: 172). The roles of dominant and submissive have become fixed, imposing rigid constraints on the behaviour of dominants in particular and leaving all the fun for the submissives. The community has become more organized and hierarchic, adapting itself to social norms in order to win acceptance (Thompson, 1991: 210–32). As with the gay community, the S/M subculture provides no guarantee of transgressive efficacy.

Whatever the limitations of S/M as a transgressive practice, it should not be equated with a death-wish, as Miller (1993: 20–32) suggests. Certainly, Foucault pursued ecstatic pleasure, a pleasure which he says 'would be so deep, so intense, so overwhelming that I couldn't survive it'. His dream was to 'die of an overdose of pleasure of any kind' (1988l: 12). A beautifully fashioned suicide could be 'the simplest of pleasures' (1979g). Did Foucault seek unbearable lightness in the form of his own death by pursuing the extreme pleasures of S/M? The question is misplaced: Foucault died of AIDS, not S/M.

Practices of the Self and Politics

A more general difficulty with Foucault's transgressive practices is that the strategy of desexualization is too narrow an approach for dealing with the ways contemporary subjects are tied to embodied identities. Sexuality, and the question of bodily desires, is only one of the features according to which whole populations are tied to racial and ethnic identities, as Foucault indicates in connection with the alleged degeneracy of Jews, who were identified with the usurious profession to which they were legally limited (1980k: 224). Different strategies of self-transgression are required for non-sexual identities. Thus, the practices of the self developed by the socialist stream of Zionism focused on constructing the 'new Jew' as a masculine agricultural pioneer in their efforts to shatter the previous identity of Diaspora Jews, as defined by anti-Semites.

Foucault's focus on personal sexual subjectivity correlates with his concern for the self. The broadest objection to Foucault's practices of transgression is that constant concern for the self induces a withdrawal from politics (Hiley, 1984: 206). Self-creation, as exemplified by Baudelaire, is a feat of individual heroism which Foucault does not reconcile with a notion of community or polity (Hiley, 1985: 77–80). Baudelaire constructs himself as a permanent critic of his era (1984c: 42), as if refusing to ever be part of a community. His heroism could be thought of not as a withdrawal from politics but as an individual artistic protest. However, the nub of the criticism here is that Foucault does not develop a concept of 'juridical subjectivity' (White, 1986: 429). He does not promote arts of the self that fashion subjects who would be capable of cooperating politically in a polity or a social movement. These would be juridical subjects because they would accept the validity of consensually and rationally chosen rules and norms. Foucault singles out Greek ethics because it 'is centered on a problem of personal choice ... without any relation to the juridical per se, with an authoritarian system, with a disciplinary structure' (1984b: 348). In this light, arts of the self can escape all social power relations and become purely personal. Greek ethics entails no normalization (341). Foucault's concern for aesthetic subjects seems to preclude concern for political subjects, and thus politics too.

Implicit in Foucault's accounts of arts of the self, however, is an argument that community and social movement do not require juridical subjects. He conceives of a gay community constructed around friendship and an S/M subculture that coheres because of a common pursuit of new pleasures (1984h). Moreover, arts of the self are not individually idiosyncratic practices. The individual has available only those technologies of the self that are in cultural circulation, and which may be imposed rather than being individually chosen (1988p: 11).[6] An art of the self must make sense to others by being embedded in shared understandings, so it can be no more purely private than a language (Rajchman, 1991: 8). Baudelaire's heroism is interpretable as aesthetic protest because of the general structure of cultural modernity that reserves a space for such protest (White, 1986: 426).[7]

Foucault's studies of Greek and Hellenist ethics illustrate the political conditions for practices of the self. He claims that government of oneself is linked to government of others. In Greek ethics, mastery of oneself, and avoiding being dominated by one's pleasures or by others, was a necessary prerequisite for hierarchic rule over others (1987b: 47, 59, 72–6, 79, 83, 170–4, 219–20). Ruling political subjects fashioned themselves through arts of the self. The shift in political conditions, from city-state to empire, called for new ethics (1984b: 357–8). Foucault rejects the view that the aristocracy's intensified cultivation of the self represented a withdrawal from politics in the imperial era. Rather, they developed a self which could cope with more complex relations of reciprocity and mutuality, in marriage as well as politics. This was achieved by conducting oneself according to universal, rational principles (1988o: 41, 80–4, 184, 238).

Foucault also implies that apparently ethical and personal concerns are still central to our political subjectivities today. Gay friendship is posited as a social relation antagonistic to the family (1984h: 30) because the polity is not constituted merely by relations between political subjects or citizens, but also by institutionalized relations, especially the family. Foucault is primarily concerned with these more basic social relations, which are closely involved with processes of subjectification. Foucault's genealogies of the subject indicate that individuals are constituted from the start in ways that correlate with social norms. The fabric of society is woven out of relations that both require certain types of individuals and more or less succeed in producing them. If Foucault is right, then attempts to resist current modes of subjection entail opposing networks of power and rationalities of government. Efforts to promote new subjectivities require that alternative modes of government be instituted by refashioning contemporary ones. Hence the promotion of new subjectivities is not merely an ethical question, but also 'political, . . . social, philosophical' (1982a: 216).

The ethical-political question has been addressed by social movements which since the 1960s have 'really changed our whole lives, our mentality, our attitudes'. This political innovation and experimentation has occurred outside the social and political programmes promoted by parties that have been with us since the nineteenth century (1984h: 58). The struggles that resist the power relations of contemporary humanist government in order to refuse current subjections are not the campaigns waged by traditional political organizations (1982a: 211–12). It is difficult to locate Foucault on the political map we have inherited from the nineteenth century, as he does not fit the categories of Marxist, anarchist, liberal, etc. (1984f: 383).

Foucault does belong to a political 'we', though this 'we' is not easily classifiable according to traditional categories. How does one define the gay movement, feminism, youth protests, the movements of ethnic and national minorities, and the diffuse discontents of clients of educational, health and welfare systems who are identified as single mothers, unemployed, or delinquent? His transgressive practices of the self with writing, drugs, gay friendship and S/M operate in the space opened by these movements. Those whose designated desires, genders, ethnic identities, or welfare categorizations to do not seem to fit resist in this space. It is the space in which some women refuse to be feminine and become feminists; in which black-skinned people refuse to be Negroes and become African-Americans; and in which men who desire other men might refuse to be homosexuals and become gay. Like Foucault, they practise the politics of those who refuse to be who they are and strive to become other.

However, the political implications of Foucault's concern for, and arts of, the self are only implicit in his theory. He even denies the potential ramifications by suggesting that new personal ethics could be pursued without affecting economic or political structures (1984b: 350). This oddly apolitical position is a consequence of Foucault's determination to separate ethics as much as possible from the axis of political power in his analysis of Greek and Hellenist arts of the self. The political significance of Foucault's turn to ethics of the self would be much clearer had he elaborated on the ways in which, even in Classical Greece but especially in the contemporary West, transformations of the self would reverberate throughout society. The religious right in the USA are keenly aware of this, which is why they oppose gay, feminist and multicultural movements. Yet the political significance of Foucault's work has not been lost on contemporary theorists, to whom I turn in the next chapter.

9

Foucault in Contemporary Political Theory

This chapter examines some of the points of contact between Foucault's political thought and other streams of contemporary theory. Contemporary feminist theory is permeated with references to Foucault, and I shall focus here on feminists who find some aspects of his thought appropriate. Jürgen Habermas has emerged as a leading figure of theory and an advocate of the brand of humanist modernism to which Foucault was opposed. Habermas and others who adopt his perspective have delivered the most telling criticisms of Foucault's project as a whole. Finally, Foucault's politics have also infused recent North American theory, often referred to as post-modernist, which is the current manifestation of a radical democratic tradition. I argue that Foucault's agonal politics are best placed within this tradition.

Feminism

Foucault identifies his politics of resistance with, among other struggles, 'opposition to the power of men over women' (1982a: 211), which is certainly one way to define feminist politics. There are several common concerns for Foucault and feminists. Martin (1988: 6, 10) points to Foucault's micro-physics of power reaching into the body and his study of normalizing institutions that affect women in particular. His reversal of the repressive hypothesis confirms feminist objections to the sexual liberation movement of the 1960s (11). Yet it is Foucault's genealogical approach which offers the most to feminist thought. His notion of power as subjectification contributes, obliquely, to the force of the feminist slogan: 'the personal is the political'. Given that the power that feminists are opposed to in the quotation above is 'a form of power which makes individuals subjects' (1982a: 212), one might expect Foucault to offer genealogies of gendered subjects. These genealogies might trace the engendering of women as passive, nurturing, emotional subjects tied to the limitations of their bodily existence and reproductive functions. They would analyse the various power/knowledge regimes and rationalities of government that constitute women as subordinated subjects or objects in relation to men. As genealogical critiques, they would pave the way for transgression of the limits that subject women.

Yet Foucault offers only a perfunctory sketch of the 'hysterization of women's bodies' (1978b: 104). He refers to the 'nervous' and 'idle' middle-class woman (121) whose educative and reproductive function as mother embedded her in key social positions and whose inherent 'pathology' made her the subject of constant medical attention (104). Foucault's sketch gives the impression that all women were subjected in the same way, as he discusses no other women. It also offers no hint that female bodies targeted by bio-power are capable of resistance (151–2, 155).

What might be needed is '*a feminist genealogy* of the category of women', of the subject whose oppression is to be ended by feminism (Butler, 1990: 5). A feminist genealogy examines those physical yet aesthetic disciplines which Foucault overlooks that produce specifically feminine bodies: dieting, exercise, dressing, cosmetics. Women internalize a male gaze which enforces norms of feminine bodily gestures, sizes, appetites and appearances. Self-surveillance provides women with a sense of what it means to be a woman, insidiously upholding patriarchy despite the absence of formal controls (Bartky, 1988). New medical reproductive technologies have concentrated on women as mothers, producing categories of women in relation to the norm of the 'fit mother' (Sawicki, 1991: 80–94). De Lauretis (1987: 2–3) proposes that we trace how images of gender are constructed through various representational technologies, such as cinema, narrative and theory. McNay (1992: 38) argues that such feminist genealogies of women, if conducted in relation to similar genealogies of masculine subjects and in historical context, would adequately overcome the shortcomings of Foucault's ungendered genealogies.

The absence of gender in Foucault's accounts of how people are consti-tuted as subjects may not be so inconsequential. Bartky (1988: 63–4) suggests that Foucault's own approach is sexist in that it assumes that male and female bodies are disciplined in the same way, although he considers only typically male disciplines. His notion of sexuality is also undifferen-tiated (de Lauretis, 1987: 14), overlooking the particular consequences for women of its deployment in the nineteenth century. Foucault is gender blind (de Lauretis, 1987: 3, McNay, 1992: 32–6), and feminists are rightly suspicious of theories that do not analyse the power relations between men and women. His alleged position that rape should be decriminalized (1988b: 200–10) can be attributed to this failure (McNay, 1992: 194–5). He does not realize that, under present conditions, to treat rape as if it were assault would in effect defend the right of rapists (de Lauretis, 1987: 36–8).

Foucault addresses issues of sexuality, which also concern feminists, through his strategy of desexualization (McNay, 1992: 194; Woodhull, 1988: 169). The general aim of this strategy of resistance is to detach people from their sexually defined identities, such as 'hysterical' women. The validity of Foucault's position for feminism rests on an argument that women in particular are constrained by oppressive sexual subjectivities. Effective desexualization requires an analysis of how sex and subjectifying power are linked, as proposed by Foucault (1978b: 103).[1] The strategy of desexualization for Foucault is thus not only a question of feminism, but of a wider resistance to our subjection primarily as sexual subjects. Hence he states that:

> The real strength of the women's movement is not that of having laid claim to the specificity of their sexuality and the rights pertaining to it, but that they have actually departed from the discourse conducted within the apparatuses of sexuality ... a veritable movement of de-sexualisation, ... formulating the demand for forms of culture ... which are no longer part of that ... pinning down to their sex (1980k: 219–20).

Foucault's position here matches his rejection of identity politics based on an essential gay subjectivity. Just as some activists argue that gay politics must be founded in this subject, so do many feminists insist that feminism rests on a metanarrative of the emancipation of the (female) subject and that its analyses of oppression require stable, ahistorical categories such as gender (McNay, 1992: 123). Many feminist political theorists adhere to the rules of humanist theory. They seek extra-political grounds for theory in notions of a subject of feminism, who is the bearer of a privileged knowledge about excesses of power. Current excesses of (male) power can be condemned as domination of the (female) subject, while a vision of a totally transformed society is projected as the realization of presently repressed subjectivity. For such feminists, Foucault's strategy of desexualization is extremely problematic, because it undermines the solidity of the female subject and thus also the grounds of feminist politics (e.g. Hartsock, 1990).

Other feminists, Butler (1990: viii–ix) among them, conceive of feminism as resistance to female subjectivities. She theorizes without appealing to extra-political grounds in order to expose the deleterious political effects of presupposing a stable subject of feminism. Butler argues that feminist genealogies would demonstrate how women are constituted as gendered subjects subordinate to men (2–7). The radical strategy for feminism, then, is not to improve the condition of women within networks of power that subject, but to subvert the constitution of women's identity. Foucault's project contributes to this task by demonstrating that sex as well as gender is culturally constructed in what Butler refers to as the heterosexual matrix. There is no aspect of identity that is extra-political, even though, according to the heterosexual matrix, sex is a natural fact. Concepts of the person or of subjectivity, which are always gendered, rely on coherence between sex, gender and sexuality (in the sense of sexual desire) (17). Foucault contributes to the disruption of the coherence of the heterosexual matrix which binds women to subjectivities that are necessarily subordinate to men.

Identity-oriented feminisms proposed by adherents of humanism are organized around supposedly common structures of oppression (14). In contrast, Butler argues for a coalition politics that would include women of different classes, cultures and sexualities who do not fit into established categories of women (5) and would itself constitute the political 'we' which is the subject of feminism (15–16). Coalition is depicted by some feminists (e.g. Reagon, 1984) as an unsafe and unsettling space in which differences have to be dealt with. It is a space fit for agonal subjects for whom difference is not something to overcome in order to establish a common identity, but a resource for resistance (Sawicki, 1988: 187). The feminist movement has had to accommodate women of different classes, races, ethnicities, religions, cultures and sexualities, which has multiplied the subject of Woman into women. As de Lauretis (1987: 2) notes, this entails generating notions of gender less bound up with sexual difference. The admission of difference in coalitions does eliminate the possibility of feminist politics organized around a single difference but reorganizes it around the varying concerns of its members.

However, Foucault's claim that the success of the women's movement derives from detachment from female identity is exaggerated. Just as gays must still fight for the rights to practise their sexuality, so must women still struggle on issues that pin them to their sex or gender: the right to control one's own body; reproductive rights (Diamond and Quinby, 1988: 194–7); equal pay for equal work; equal opportunities in careers and education; welfare provision for maternity leave, single mothers, etc. These unfinished struggles are undertaken by women as women and for women. As Sawicki (1991: 105–6) remarks, women may well have to rely more on the capacities for resistance they have been endowed with as constrained subjects than would a white male such as Foucault. The effectiveness of desexualization as a strategy to reduce domination of women would be limited to (yet also as extensive as) those areas of gender inequality in which sexuality has been deployed.

As do many other political theorists, some feminists portray Foucault as a pessimistic prophet of entrapment (Alcoff, 1990: 74–5; Hartsock, 1990: 167). In contrast, feminists who make critical use of Foucault's work are adept at indicating potentialities for resistance in his approach. For example, the key point Sawicki (1991: 108) takes up from Foucault is that the constraining limitations that subject one as a woman are also the enabling limits that empower one with the capacities of a subject who resists (55–6). These feminists are also more sensitive to the incoherencies of power relations than Foucault. Butler (1990: 17) points to the persistence of identities that do not conform to the established coherence of sex, gender and sexuality. De Lauretis (1987: 3) suggests that the excess of gender ideology opens it to contestation, in so far as women can never match themselves to its representations (10). Without being able to transcend the limits of gender ideology, critique occurs at the margins of discourses and in the 'chinks and cracks' of power/knowledge regimes (25).

There is always something of Foucault's 'plebs' in women, that is, always something that does not quite fit the allotted subjectivity. Freud realized that the transition to adult heterosexuality is much more precarious for women than men. This does not make women relatively freer, however, as the failure of power incites medical, psychoanalytic and cultural interventions. Feminists using Foucault's work are sensitive to the ways in which women who do not fit the mould provoke further exercises of power. As Butler (1990: 105–6) argues, the hermaphrodite whose memoirs Foucault published and commented on (1980m) is studied, judged and effectively driven to suicide. Female anorexics rebel against both traditional female domestic roles and contrasting images of women as hungrily and voraciously demanding by practising inordinate control over their bodies in order to remain boys (Bordo, 1988). Rather than escaping female subjectivity, they incite further medical intervention and the perpetuation of representations of women as neurotic, being the heirs of Victorian hysterical women (105). In other words, the theorists mentioned above resist Foucault's temptations to regard resistance as the transgression of all limits. The problem is always how to work on and with the limits of the present.

In this light, the complicity of women in their own subjection becomes a resource. Butler (1990: 24–5), building on the position that engendered subjects do not simply exist but are constituted, conceives of gender as constant performance: 'gender proves to be performative, constituting the identity it is purported to be'. Gendered subjects are always in a state of becoming, rather than being. 'Gender is the repeated stylization of the body' which has congealed so much that it appears natural (33). Genealogy exposes the contingency of what appears natural, enabling one to loosen the ties to one's identity. While Foucault recognizes that enabling limits empower subjects to resist being who they are, he gives the impression that identities become fixed without having to be constantly maintained. Butler adds the insight that agency is required of each subject to sustain identity by constantly repeating it (145). Given that subjections are not final but must be constantly repeated, the feminist question is how to perform gender in a way that subverts gender identity (31–2).

Butler's suggestive answer is that identity is subverted through parodic performance that exposes the absence of an original or essential gender identity which can be copied (31, 137–8). 'Cultural practices such as drag, cross-dressing, and the sexual stylization of butch/femme identities' (137) parody the notion of the heterosexual original and thereby subvert the stability of what now only appear to be substantive gendered identities (141). Foucault (implicitly) and Butler (explicitly) argue for a feminist politics whose 'we' is not the representation of women's given identities and the interests attached to them (Butler 1990: 142, 149). They both assert that political collectivities and movements rest not on extra-political justifications and foundations, but on action and practice.

Neither Butler nor Foucault necessarily have the fail-safe strategy for feminist or gay politics. Tyler (1991) argues that drag and gender-parody in general can easily be reinscribed into the models they are supposed to subvert. In the absence of a context that makes it clear that parody is parody and not imitation of natural gender, the performer's intentions are overwhelmed by all those forces that generally conceal how gender is invented. Similarly, Bersani (1988: 207–9) suspects that gay machismo images have less to do with parodic subversion and more to do with sexual excitement generated by masculinity. Nonetheless, certain approaches to feminist politics can make critical use of Foucault's work. The mottoes of such feminism would be very similar to Foucault's politics: 'Take care of yourself by styling yourself subversively; know yourself through a critical practice that reveals the limits of your gendered subjectivity by transgressing those limits; ground feminist politics not in imagined female essence, not in privileged feminine knowledge, not in a stable woman's identity, but in the action of a coalition of those who are also called women and accept that identity as they seek to overcome it.'

Foucault and Habermas

Foucault and Habermas are frequently considered to oppose each other, not least because Habermas (1983: 14) condemned Foucault as a postmodernist 'Young Conservative' enemy of the project of modernity. Yet there is much that connects them. Both were haunted by the Third Reich. Foucault experienced his early years under the menace of the rise of fascism and Nazism (1988l: 6–7) and his adolescence in Occupation France as 'an absolutely threatening world' (cited in Megill, 1985: 246). Habermas's work is also inspired by the fear that political forms of irrationality, like Nazism, might resurface in Europe (Richters, 1988: 616, 621). Both thinkers are also aware of a paradox at the root of modern Western politics. Foucault maintains that the main characteristic of modern political rationality is the constant correlation of individualization and totalization (1988k: 161–2). Habermas (1984: 289) points out that social welfare policies are designed to countervail the negative effects of wage labour production, not only materially but by securing freedom in the face of market forces. However, the legal-bureaucratic form of welfare organization cancels out whatever autonomy the policies offer. Thus both free-market liberalism and its social democratic alleviation undermine subjective capacities of agency at the same time as they provide the space or material resources for it. Habermas (1987: 291) thus argues that in welfare-state democracies 'it is the legal means for securing freedom that themselves endanger freedom'. It is a dilemma that individual freedom and autonomy can be gained only at the cost of greater regulation. Moreover, both thinkers look favourably on similar social movements that resist what Habermas refers to as the colonization of the life world (its invasion by instrumental rationality) and Foucault as normalization (White, 1986: 422–3).

However, Habermas and Foucault have quite different responses to the dangers and dilemmas of modernity. Foucault wishes to salvage the philosophical ethos of enlightenment as permanent critique which he attributes to Kant (1984c: 49–50). In doing so, he insists on separating the ethos of enlightenment from humanism and associated forms of modern power. Habermas's (1983) concern is to complete the project of modernity, which entails overcoming the dilemma of modernity by subjecting modernization processes, which include oppressive economic and bureaucratic features, to normative, universal, consensual, intersubjective communicative reason. Habermas's (1984) argument is that in all communicative action implicit appeals are made to universal validity claims that delineate procedures for resolving disagreements by appealing to intersubjective understandings about what counts as a good argument (about what is true, right or beautiful). Communicative reason is the elaboration of this background and is exemplified by the ideal speech situation in which agreement between equals is completely uncoerced. Every social situation can be measured against this regulative ideal, which can be embodied in juridical rules that limit excesses of power and provide freedom.

Habermas's communicative reason is intended to integrate other modes of modernist reason whose detachment from each other has ruptured modernity (234–41). Cognitive-instrumental rationality refers to scientific knowledge which enables the human subject to achieve its ends while relating to the world (including even one's body) as external objects. Moral-practical reason refers to the autonomous selection of ends by the subject. While much of the criticism by Habermas's precursors in the Frankfurt School and by Weber focused on the expansion of instrumental at the expense of moral reason, Habermas is also concerned that disconnected moral reason leads isolated subjects to assert themselves regardless of others. The third, aesthetic-expressive sphere, is concerned with the authenticity of expressions of emotion and sensation, which also tends towards self-assertion in isolation from the other two spheres.

Habermas systematizes Weber's account of the rationalization of religious world-views into three autonomous spheres which pursue their own logic in competition with each other and are institutionalized in different orders of life. Weber was himself drawing on a Kantian tradition, so that Habermas's trisection replicates the structure of Kant's three critiques of the conditions of possibility for the different types of judgement we make – aesthetic, scientific and moral. Habermas accepts that each of the three value spheres has its own validity claims (truth, rightness and authenticity) and that each serves a valid and necessary human interest. We need to control the world, to determine goals rationally and to express ourselves. However, in isolation the pursuit of each interest becomes the irrational assertion of the subject. Rather than sinking into Weber's pessimism about the inevitable disenchantment of the life world caused by the detachment of value spheres, Habermas proposes a more inclusive notion of reason that both integrates the validity claims of each of the three spheres and replaces the destructive philosophy of the subject with a normative model of consensual, cooperative intersubjectivity in which others are not treated as objects but respected as equal interlocutors. Autonomy can be attained only in solidarity with others.

Habermas (1987) criticizes Foucault from several angles, all of which lead to the conclusion that Foucault's total critique of reason is incoherent because it relies paradoxically on the very structure of rationality it opposes. Foucault's critique is particularly partial in so far as it is inspired by aesthetic modernism (275, 285–6), whose critical standards are derived from the unspoken language of the body in pain (284). Although this tradition identifies rationalization as the enemy, the autonomy of its aesthetic discourse rests on the rationalized differentiation of the life world into three spheres.

Arguing from a Habermassian perspective, White (1986) agrees with Foucault that during the process of modernization these aspects of our lives have been devalued. Cognitive, scientific truth claims have 'colonized' the interactive, normative and aesthetic authenticity claims. Correspondingly, the scientific-technological sphere of life predominates over the moral-practical and aesthetic-expressive ones. On the one hand, White argues, Habermas is sensitive to the pre-rational other, recognizing an imbalance, which must be corrected, between the scientific-technological, moral-practical and the aesthetic-expressive spheres in modern society. On the other hand, Foucault wants to extend the aesthetic sphere to cover the others, armed only with an ethics defined as a relationship to the self. In general, while Foucault's critics may accept that art expresses some legitimate protest against exclusion of human creative and libidinal qualities, they cannot accept what Habermas (1983: 12) calls the terrorist over-extension of the aesthetic cultural order into domains such as politics.

In Habermas's scheme, the full pursuit of aesthetic lifestyles and of absolute expressive authenticity is a form of protest against disenchantment. As protest, aesthetic thought can correct some excessive features of modernization, but cannot provide the foundations for an alternative conception of society and politics. Art must be limited to its proper bounds because it is incapable of producing stable forms of social life. Aesthetic rationality functions well according to its inner logic when it expresses natural beauty or authentic needs and desires. But as there is no aesthetic logic of social interaction, counter-cultural forms of life such as Bohemianism are unstable, having to rely on other values (Habermas,1984: 238–9). Foucault's critique, too, implicitly relies on the values of rational modernity which he opposes. However, Habermas's reading of Foucault's aesthetics is too narrow, as the latter's approach has little to do with the expression of authenticity and much more to do with the action entailed by the creative process of self-fashioning. Such self-fashioning operates without reference to an authentic original or essence which has been discovered, and as self-conscious invention.

Habermas also considers Foucault's critique to be contradictory with respect to the truth claims of his work. The archaeological and genealogical knowledge Foucault produces in order to demonstrate that the will to knowledge is itself a will to power is prone to self-referentialism. In other words, Foucault's critique must itself represent a will to power (247–8). Habermas assumes that a successful radical critique must itself be extra-political or innocent of such complicity. He reads Foucault's genealogy as an account of the insinuation of evil power into good truth, while suggesting that Foucault considered his own work to be superior to the human sciences (268–81). Yet Foucault avoids the problem of self-referentialism by recognizing the complicity of his knowledge in networks of power and resistance, its incompleteness, its fictional character and most importantly its amenability to challenge.

Another angle of Habermas's criticism is that Foucault lacks normative foundations which would enable him to judge some power formations illegitimate and thus justify resistance. He cites Fraser (1981: 283), who asks why domination ought to be resisted. Given that Foucault is not neutral about forms of power, then 'What Foucault needs and needs desperately are normative criteria for distinguishing acceptable from unacceptable forms of power' (286). Fraser argues that the force of Foucault's argument presupposes the liberal norms he criticizes (284), while Habermas (1987: 282–4) concurs that Foucault is a cryptonormativist who makes familiar complaints about asymmetries of power. However, while Foucault is neutral toward power itself because it has both enabling and constraining forms, he does prefer forms of power that allow for agonism. In this way, Foucault may well satisfy Fraser's (1985: 180) demand for an 'appeal to some alternative, posthumanist, ethical paradigm'.[2]

Habermas (1987: 276–81), however, would insist that whatever norms

Foucault adopts, he must argue why they are better than the humanist ones he rejects. In doing so, he implicitly appeals to universal validity claims regarding the consensual, non-coercive nature of proper argumentation. If, on the other hand, Foucault makes no arguments but relies on the effects of his work to promote resistance, he falls into the self-referentialist trap again because his counter-discourses are nothing else than the effects of power they unleash, just like the humanist discourses Foucault attacks.

The nub of the difficulty here is that Habermas and Foucault diverge greatly in their perceptions of discourse, knowledge and argumentation. Habermas maintains that the paradigmatic human practice of linguistic communication contains an ideal of human relations free from power in the sense of domination but also of strategic manipulation of others. Foucault (1982a: 217–18, 1988j: 18; 1993: 203) acknowledges Habermas's conceptual differentiation of techniques of signs or communication and techniques of domination, of the self, and of production. However, he insists that power relations permeate all other relations (1978b: 94; 1980h: 142). If Foucault were to include techniques of communication in his genealogical critiques, it would not be as an autonomous domain but as another analytical axis that interferes and is interfered with by the practices of the other axes (1982a: 218; 1984f: 386). Foucault is wary of the attainment of consensus as a regulative principle (1984e: 379) and rejects the ideal of communication uncontaminated by power as utopian (1988p: 18). Reason is always impure.

Habermas's (1987: 297) model of human relations is one of 'linguistically generated intersubjectivity', or non-adversarial dialogue and mutual respect. Foucault's model is one of agonistic and strategic interaction in which respect for others is based in their resistance to attempts to govern their conduct (1982a: 225). Habermas envisages freedom as practice devoid of power, whereas Foucault identifies liberty as the practice of power. In Habermas's world valid claims would be recognized as such by rational interlocutors, whereas Foucault's *parrhesiast* accepts the risks of criticizing those in power. His notion of political discourse resembles the model of a Greek *polis*, in which public speakers wrestle with each others' arguments in order to determine policy. For Habermas (1987: 272–6) a model based on strategic relations is one in which subjects manipulate objects, so that he reads Foucault's genealogies as accounts of objectification of people rather than subjectification. Only communicative interaction in which subjects accept common procedures of argumentation enables them to recognize each other as equals because they are the same. For Foucault, it is the irreducibility of others to one's strategies that teaches one to respect others as free subjects because they are different.

Habermas aims to complete the project of modernity by simultaneously healing the diremptions of reason and social domination. But what is the cost of Habermas's attempt to resolve the dilemma of modernity? He proposes that potentially repressive legal regulations be subject to critique by communicative rationality. In this way bureaucratic-administrative rationalization can be held in check by emancipatory reason. Habermas (296) rightly argues that Foucault is too dismissive of the potential of juridical norms to obstruct disciplinary norms. Yet if Foucault's account of modernity is one-sided in this way, Habermas's rendition underplays its dangers. His recognition of the paradox of modernity contains no hint of its costly and tragic qualities (Agnes Heller, cited in McNay, 1992: 188) or its ambiguity (Connolly, 1985: 374).

Foucault, focusing not on modernity in general but on its humanism and political rationality, finds not a reconcilable problem but an 'antinomy between law and order' that reflects the antinomy of individualization and totalization (1988k: 162). Reconciliations of law as the juridical system and order as the state's administrative system always favour the latter. Excessive, rationalized order can be resisted not merely because there are still philosophically grounded juridical norms that do not articulate easily with disciplinary norms, but because of the oppositional practices of those who employ the resources available in their present, some of which are relics from the past. Foucault's approach is attentive to those who pay the price of the antinomy of humanism.

Habermas's reliance on philosophical defences against irrational politics entails another cost implicit in his critique of Foucault. Nihilistic political paralysis ensues when theorists who demand philosophical reasons to resist and extra-political criteria for judging good from bad forms of power are confronted by the absence of such grounds. Fraser (1985: 178–80) confronts an imaginary 'sophisticated Habermassian humanist' with Foucault's claim that the constitution of subjects occurs as much through apparently autonomous self-subjection as through oppressive subjection by others. The problem then is not, as Habermas suggests, that humans are objectified and that power is asymmetrical and hierarchical, but that humanist appeals to autonomy and reciprocity can be integrated into humanist subjection. She argues that the Habermassian should 'concede that these humanist notions have no critical force with respect to the fully panopticized society', but should also 'claim that this is no objection to them, since there is no *good reason* to oppose such a society' (emphasis added). What Foucault would describe as a fully normalized society, or a state of complete domination, could also be described as Habermas's well-ordered consensual society in which autonomy and solidarity are intertwined. In the absence of good, normative reasons on Foucault's part, Fraser opts for Habermas.

Fraser's argument demonstrates the potential for political paralysis when philosophy is allotted the task of determining which practices of power and resistance are legitimate. Significantly, Habermas (1979: 178–81) wishes to reserve this legitimating function for political philosophy as an extra-political discourse. Yet, as we have seen, the supposedly extra-political legitimation of political philosophy tends to reinforce the state's order more than the liberty of free subjects. In doing so, it also disempowers non-intellectuals who may feel the need to resist but are unable to justify themselves before the judicial authority of the state and academy. No doubt this would disallow the racist irrationalism to which Habermas most strongly objects. Yet what happens to all those others who cannot articulate the reasons for their resistance in terms he would accept? What do we do with people whom we do not respect because they seem to be irrational, and thus opposed to what we are, as rational subjects? What price do we pay for applying communicative rationalities of government to ourselves? There are inevitable costs involved in the project of modernity which Habermas conceals.

Radical Liberal Democracy

This book concludes with a discussion of how Foucault's political thought contributes to a radical transformation of liberal democratic theory. In light of Foucault's onslaught against humanism, it may seem odd to argue that his agonal politics are best encapsulated by radicalized liberal democracy. After all, liberal political thought appears to be founded on the presupposition of a sovereign, rational, autonomous individual subject. Yet, if one distinguishes Foucault's opposition to humanism from his attitude to modernity, radical liberal democracy constitutes the appropriate political conditions of possibility for his aesthetics of existence. Foucault suggests as much himself when he says that 'liberation is sometimes the political or historical condition for a practice of liberty' (1988p: 3). Is it not the presence of liberal regimes which make possible the practice of liberty?

Foucault and Mill

In this light, it may be useful to compare Foucault with J.S. Mill. The latter's sensitivity to the danger of social as well as political tyranny demonstrates awareness that power is exercised not only by sovereign authority and through the law, but also operates by means of social conformity. There is a parallel here with Foucault's rejection of juridical notions of power and his dread of normalization. What is of most interest is that Mill grasps that society has a tendency to demand specific forms of individuality or subjectivity, to 'fetter the development, and, if possible, prevent the formation, of any individuality not in harmony with its ways, and compel all characters to fashion themselves upon the model of its own ways' (Mill, 1975: 9).

Among the liberties that Mill demands for the individual are those of 'tastes and pursuits; of framing the plan of our life to suit our own character' (18). He is interested in a society in which there are 'different experiments of living', arguing that 'he who chooses his plan for himself, employs all his faculties' (70, 73), presumably including aesthetic faculties. When Mill looks for examples of 'experiments of living', which translate into Foucauldian vocabulary as aesthetics of the self, he also turns to the Greeks and Christians. Mill saw worth in both pagan self-assertion and Christian self-denial, wanting to balance a Greek ideal of self-development with a Platonic, Christian ideal of self-government. Mill, like Foucault, wanted to ensure that people had the freedom to fashion their lives as they wanted and to resist the models of subjectivity that society tries to impose on them.

As well as arguing for forms of individual liberty that resemble Foucault's aesthetics of existence, Mill also discusses the political framework and institutions he believes necessary to ensure liberty. These guarantees of liberty are embodied in practices of liberty which sustain fluid strategic relations in which agonal subjectivity can flourish. Democratic elections replace or circulate those who hold office. Policies are changed, laws rewritten, and even the boundaries of community can be altered depending on who are considered citizens. Participatory models of democracy offer more arenas for agonistic contest between political subjects. Is it not then a liberal democratic polity that is implicit in Foucault's political thought?

The answer is both yes and no. Foucault renounces the humanist political rationality of actually existing liberalism, yet his thought leads not to a total condemnation of liberalism, but to transgressive work on its limits. One of these limits is that liberal modes of subjectification are trapped in the double of individualization and totalization. 'The figure of the person is an historical innovation consequent upon a series of "liberal" transformations of "police"' (Minson, 1985: 145). Another limit is that, as a political rationality, actually existing liberalism puts its trust in philosophically justified juridical defences of individual liberty. According to this rationale, constitutions and rights make practices of liberty possible, as they guarantee basic freedoms of speech, assembly and association. The solidity of liberal bulwarks, threatened by government encroachment, corporate interests and popular enthusiasm, characterizes such liberalism. However, the effects of liberal political arrangements that are also solid, congealed and resistant to change represent another set of limits. These effects include unequal distributions of power, wealth and opportunities along lines that parallel identities to which people are tied, according to gender, sexuality, class, ethnicity, sexual orientation, religion and race. Those in subordinate positions within power relations experience dissonance between liberal presuppositions of autonomy and responsibility and their ability to change their own lives. Yet even those who enjoy the benefits of the states of domination that permeate existing liberal regimes are tied to subjectivities that offer no more than the illusion of self-fashioning.

From a Foucauldian perspective, existing liberal democracy is a system for the regulation of the self in which there is symmetry between the goals of self-fulfilment and political values of consumption, profit and social order. Modern organizations specialize in the management of subjectivity and the engineering of human souls (Rose, 1990: 1–2, 11). The entrepreneurial self constitutes itself through a series of consumer choices taken with as much and as little freedom as the supermarket shopper has and with as much autonomy from the subjecting governmental practices of capitalism as the consumer has from the market. Actually existing liberal democracy might be a necessary condition for aesthetics of the self, but it is also the sufficient condition for the forms of subjection targeted by Foucault's oppositional politics. It reduces conceptions of self-constitution to questions of self-discovery or self-selection and realization of the potential of that which is discovered or chosen. Its humanist limits preclude the attainment of agonal subjectivity.

Liberalism assumes that philosophically grounded juridical rules are adequate conditions for the freedom of the autonomous self. This faith that limits can be set to prevent excesses of power rests on deeper assumptions that the subject is essentially free and, in the normal run of affairs, is endowed (by nature or through socialization) with the rational, cognitive and creative capacities that an active subject requires. Typically, liberalism focuses on the defence of negative liberty and presupposes a pre-existing free subject. However, 'society' is a set of forces that constitute subjects in ways that can be more or less constraining, as well as more or less enabling. The deeper problem is how the power relations and limits necessary to any society can be arranged to enable and empower subjects who fashion themselves and their polity by constantly reworking those limits. This requires a radicalized liberal democratic theory.

Foucault and Connolly

The implications of Foucault's thought for radical liberal democracy are being most extensively developed by Bill Connolly. In his own terms, Connolly illustrates the political ramifications of our attachments to our identities as well as the detrimental effects of the articulation of individual with collective identity in accordance with modern political rationality. Connolly's (1993a: xxi) approach draws on Nietzsche as much as Foucault to arrive at his own formulations of a notion of militant, agonistic deterritorialized liberal democracy. Rather than proposing alternative institutions and policies, Connolly (1993b: 379) argues that Foucault's ethical sensibility corresponds to a new democratic ethos.

Much of Connolly's (1991a) attention is devoted to the issue of identity, corresponding to Foucault's concerns with subjectification. However, Connolly's presentation is far more attentive to the tension that remains implicit in Foucault's work between the unbearable lightness of unlimited subjectivity and the unbearable heaviness of constrained subjection. Identity for Connolly is always a set of limits or density that enables selves to choose, think and act (9, 64, 94). Connolly finds a paradox in the necessity that identities can be constituted and maintained only in relation to that from which they differ. In order to have a certain subjectivity one cannot have others. Recognition of this inevitable loss is repressed by taking particular identities to be inevitable because they correspond unambiguously with an ontology, or conception of the world and the place of humans in it (162–3). Identities are held to be true in so far as the world is predisposed to fit the purposes of human subjects thus defined (29–30). There is an Augustinian imperative not only to have an identity but to secure it by conceiving of it as deep, true and moral in contrast to the immorality of others (Connolly, 1993a: xvii). There is a constant temptation to defend the solidity of one's identity by conceiving of what is different as other, and of the other as evil (Connolly, 1991a: 64).

The other is cast as evil because it is the source of what Nietzsche calls resentment. In Connolly's account, resentment arises because the very existence of the other is an affront to one's solidity (66). It is a reminder that one need not be who one is, that one's identity is contingent, and that the world is not predisposed to human purposes (32). The deep root of existential resentment is human finitude, which is experienced as a fundamental unfairness that life must end before all its possibilities have been explored (164). Some agent must be responsible for evil as fundamental unfairness (1). Hegemonic identities protect themselves by marginalizing, demeaning and dominating the evil others. The necessity of limits to life and recognition of finitude arouse resentment that being is not light and unlimited. In reaction, given subjectivities and life in general are posited as heavy or thoroughly constrained by human, natural, rational or divine purpose. This heaviness is not overtly regarded as constraint, but as full recompense for finitude that makes life and its burdens meaningful.

Explicitly, Connolly (1991a: 112–13) reframes Foucault's distinctions between normal and abnormal, rational and irrational, between healthy and sick in terms of good and evil. In Connolly's version, subjectification occurs through what Foucault refers to as 'dividing practices' that establish distinctions of identity (1982a: 208). In his genealogies of identities, Connolly (1991a) contraposes Western Christians with indigenous pagans of the New World in the sixteenth century (36–45); anti-Semite and Jew (98–106); heterosexuals and homosexuals (75); or modernist priests and postmodernist heretics (58–63, 144).

As Connolly focuses on discursive practices of differentiation, his account overlooks the many techniques of subjectification that do not rely primarily on contradistinction from the other. His point that such techniques require forgetfulness or concealment of the paradox of identity is well taken

(Connolly, 1991b: 471). For example, Greek elite self-subjectification conveniently forgot women, slaves and foreigners. Yet Connolly's focus leaves him without notions of transgressive practices of the self whereby we could detach ourselves from current identities (Connolly, 1991a: 9). His main resource for recognizing contingencies of identity is reflective, historical genealogy (176, 181). He is vulnerable to his own charge that, in the absence of techniques of the self, genealogical reflection would fuel resentment in those who feel robbed of their stable identities (Connolly, 1993b: 372–3). Connolly's approach is philosophical rather than practical.

On the other hand, Connolly is more sophisticated than Foucault in that he distinguishes between necessary or existential injustice inherent in the human condition and systemic or social injustice which could be removed if the existing order were transformed (Connolly, 1991a: 34). Each set of injustices generates resentment, but existential resentment can be subdued only by cultivating a new sensibility that cares for contingent identities. Connolly is more adept than Foucault at theorizing the difficulties that would remain even if the current modern humanist order were transformed. In Connolly's terms, when Foucault is tempted to unbearable lightness he projects resentment of the present regime onto resentment of human finitude. Connolly suggests that, in order to confront the second form, the 'surplus' resentment caused by present social conditions be subdued through social transformation (211–12).

Connolly tackles the antinomy of humanist political rationality, which Foucault addresses as the combination of individualizing pastoral power with totalizing power of the state (1981f: 227), by drawing out some of the connections between the 'realism' of international relations theory and the 'idealism' of liberal democratic political theory. Liberal democratic political theory looks to the good of its citizens, whereas international relations theory looks to the good of the state in a competitive environment. Connolly (1991a: 198–9) suggests that the combination occurs by connecting personal and collective identity. Much of the former is derived from the social commonality that constitutes the latter, while one's membership of a given culture also posits one as a political subject in a territorially defined state (Connolly, 1991b: 463–4). He argues that the shared understandings of democratic politics are secured by constructing demarcations of who belongs and who does not (471–3). The self-assuredness of closed democratic identity can be sustained only by producing others as enemies who threaten the security of the democratic regime as a whole (Connolly, 1993b: 379–80).

Just as Foucault seeks to detach us from individual subjectivities, so does Connolly aim to estrange us from collective identities. The latter rest not only on unjustified exclusions, but on the viability of the sovereignty of a territorially defined state (Connolly 1991a: 30). In the democratic setting of political accountability, the state becomes 'the ultimate agency of self-conscious political action' (201). The experience of individual freedom is thus bound to the collective freedom of state action (199). Yet there is much dissonance between the image of the sovereign democratic state exercising its democratic will and the actual efficacy of the state (206). Connolly ascribes this suppressed discrepancy to 'the *globalization of contingency*' (24), by which he means the proliferation of ecological, economic, demographic and political forces that exceed the power of any state. These affronts to the self-assurance of the sovereign state provoke collective egoism which is embodied in a series of disciplinary crusades against external and internal enemies, such as terrorists and welfare cases. The state becomes the agent of generalized resentment (204–10). Collective sovereign identity is both not viable and oppressive.

Together with the critique of actually existing liberal democracy comes an elaboration of an agonistic democratic sensibility that Connolly (1993b: 365) discerns in Foucault. Foucault is credited with countering ontologies which hold that the world is predisposed to human purposes with an '*ontalogy*' (374–6). Rather than there being a fundamental logic to the world with which identities neatly harmonize, the only logics or orderings in the world are those which we impose on it for our convenience. We should not therefore be resentful that life exceeds our orderings and that we cannot pursue all of its possibilities. Connolly proposes an '*ethic of cultivation* ... of care for the contingency of things' (383). Agonistic democracy is not characterized by alternative institutions and policies (although these would presumably be needed to deal with the 'surplus' resentment caused by social inequalities). It is instead marked by a different cultural sensibility that recognizes the ambiguity of democratic regimes that also generate misfits (Connolly, 1991a: 196). Agonistic democracy is infused with a certain spirit that affirms contest between different modes of life (211).

In place of the demonization of others, Connolly anticipates agonistic respect for other identities. The cultivation of care for difference can convert antagonism into agonism in which the other is respected for revealing the limits that enable one to be who one is (178–84). Others are then seen to be living out the possibilities and some of the richness of life that we had to forego in order to be who we are (Connolly, 1991a: 159–66). Respect is based on indebtedness to those who prevent limits from congealing by sustaining the contest between different ideas, identities and policies (Connolly, 1993b: 382–3). The point, then, is not to abolish identity (or subjectivity) but to transform the way in which we experience identity. Connolly suggests that we accept the necessity of some limits without either resenting them as unbearably heavy or conceiving them as necessary.

Connolly proposes that democratic identifications be detached from the territorial state and the collective understandings located in it (380). This accords with Foucault's strategy to 'liberate us both from the state and from the type of individualization which is linked to the state' (1982a: 216). Connolly (1993b: 383) does not deny that collective identities are necessary for political action nor that all such identities tend to congeal. Like Foucault, he prefers to shift allegiances to cross-national democratic social movements which scramble demarcations of the cosy inside of democratic politics and the hazardous outside of inter-state conflicts (Connolly, 1991b: 478–9).

Yet the cultural, ethical sensibility of agonistic democracy can never be securely achieved (Connolly, 1993b: 378). We are always in revolt against the unbearable lightness of being in which all is contingent, nothing necessary (375). Agonistic democracy thus cultivates a *'politics of disturbance'* (Connolly, 1991b: 473). An ethic of permanent resistance is required because the limits needed to give form to self, thought and community tend to solidify and congeal. Democracy, if infused with this sensibility, is the appropriate political framework because it institutionalizes agonal contests that disturb theories, identities, policies and constitutions. Differences that challenge the limits of who we are, what we think and what we may hope for are, in an agonistic democracy, vital dangers without which the polity would solidify along the lines of its current limits. In Foucault's terms, the possibilities for strategic engagements that stave off systems of domination are held open when practices of liberty are institutionalized.

A radicalized liberal polity that affirms agonal subjectivity would aim at openness and temporality of its constitution, laws, policies and identity. It would institute participatory practices that encourage activism and engagement in political contest. In other words, a good part of the enthusiasm for liberty which Kant felt to be embodied in revolutions that overthrew tyranny must be sustained in everyday politics (1986b: 93–6). One reason for this is that: 'The liberty of men is never assured by the institutions and laws that are intended to guarantee them . . . The guarantee of freedom is freedom' (1984g: 245). Conventional liberalism acknowledges political struggle only as a prerequisite of freedom from tyranny, whereas Foucault values struggles as liberty which opens up and preserves political freedoms (Thiele, 1990: 922). There is a negative aspect of liberty, which prevents the congealment of liberal laws and institutions that results in fixed, unequal power relations and closes down strategic possibilities. A Foucauldian defence of liberal freedoms would argue that rights are conditions of possibility for the practice of liberty, which has to be undertaken daily in order to create free individuals.

Liberal democracy can be radicalized theoretically by liberating it from its philosophical foundations and assumptions about already existing autonomous subjectivity. Stagnation debilitates liberalism when its practices are thought to embody static and universal truths and reason. Both individualist and communitarian liberal theories tend towards closure and solidification of the boundaries and institutions of their polities.[3] The drive to stabilize the achievements of liberal revolutions forecloses options for the ongoing practice of liberty that extends and alters those achievements. As Foucault complains, the urge is always towards order.

In contrast, radicalized liberal democracy embraces aesthetics of existence on a political as well as an individual level. It requires a shift away from the habit of conceiving and constructing politics from models of deduction of rational principles, of social regularities empirically discovered, and of the hermeneutical interpretation of embedded communal values.[4] According to these models, the polity is fashioned as if it were a mimetic representation of reason, reality or community, each conceived as stable originals. Such political theories occlude both their own nature, as arts of politics that construct rather than copy, and the absence of the original they appear to copy.

An aesthetics of political existence fashions the polity without reference to an original and without imitating the truth of human nature, rational principles, social regularities or communal authenticity. It creates political fictions with self-conscious awareness that it does so, while also being aware that the political 'facts' created by other theories are also fictions. It confronts agonal subjects with an awesome responsibility: to style their polity in the absence of predefined limitations. The absence of absolute limits, which in conventional liberal theory are supposed to prevent excesses of power, makes aesthetics of political existence dangerous. It also offers the greatest opportunities for freedom. The risk and the promise are necessary conditions for each other.

Conclusion

Foucault's political thought is timely in ways that are not immediately obvious. The concern for 'cultural' issues of identity politics and concern for the self, rather than allegedly 'real' issues of economics and social distribution should not be considered the luxury of the rich. Politics that centres on the identities of social groups converges with issues such as the feminization of poverty and ethnic inequalities. Nor are these by any means merely Western concerns. It is precisely the conjuncture of struggles to control scarce resources with ethnic and national conflicts in Eastern Europe and the former Soviet Union that makes cultural and identity politics all too real. Conventional politics today, focusing on economic processes and classes, is woefully inadequate to deal with conflicts waged over 'who we are', just as it was earlier in the century (1991: 59). Perhaps there is no more pressing political need than arts of the self through which people detach themselves from current subjectivities. Foucault's thought is therefore timely because it addresses the costs of remaining attached to seemingly natural personal and collective identities. It challenges modern political rationality which ties personal identity and the empowerment of the individual with the enhancement of the power of a territorially defined political totality.

Foucault's thought is also timely because it is an internal critique of our present that proceeds without proposing a viable alternative system. For more than a century, actually existing liberalism has had to legitimate itself in the face of socialist critiques claiming to offer better social systems. Given the decline of the socialist alternatives, there is the distinct danger that actually existing liberal democracy will become increasingly dogmatic in the absence of credible challenges. Liberal democracy is losing the spirits of the revolutions that constituted it, along with the enthusiasm that Kant discerned as a sign of hope in his time. Foucault's is a critical thought for a Western present without an alternative.

Foucault (1988h: 155) recognizes that transformation requires the disturbance of our deepest cultural assumptions about ourselves and our world. Overtly political programmes of transformation hope that people will change if the system is reorganized. Foucault implies that political systems change when people do. Transgressive work on the limits of the present is a practical as well as an intellectual task. His own experiments in transgressing the limits of himself and his present are precisely experiments (1984e: 374), not blueprints for success. He leaves us with no prescriptions or formulae to transgress our limits, but with a body of passionate writing, ranging from the anguished passion of *Madness and Civilization* (1965), to the militant passion of his condemnations of humanism, to the austere passion of his last books on care of oneself.

Foucault's passion is for a politics that embraces what cannot be finalized and what cannot be solved. The politics implicit in his thought would encompass the two poles to which he was tempted: unbearable lightness and unbearable heaviness. Just as the tension between these two poles is necessary to sustain his thought as its condition of possibility, so is it necessary for his agonal politics. It is the contest between these two urges, the one seeking a site of untrammelled freedom beyond all limits and the other the safety of life rendered meaningful by its inescapable limits, that defines the limits of agonal politics.

Foucault provides no prescription of what is to be done, but he does offer theoretical guidelines for the formation of new subjectivities and communities: take care of yourself; untie ethical self-formation from scientific knowledge and moral codes; do not be more true to what you are now (gay, a woman, Hispanic, Serbian), but detach yourself from your identity and become someone other; do not be overwhelmed by the unbearable heaviness of your humanist present, but look for its disarticulations, the points where it is a little out of joint and provokes excesses that resist it; but do not be tempted to seek life without limits, a subjectivity without any identity, or a society without power. Foreswear the dream of a perfect world in which all has been done and all is safe, but cherish the agonism of open strategic games in which everything remains to be done. Love your liberty, which you have when you can act and do so. Take care of yourself; know 'yourself' by transgressing your limits; practise liberty.

Notes

1 Introduction

1. See 1982c: 190, where Foucault argues that Wagner's mythology is still very much alive for Europeans in the late twentieth century.

2. I borrow the notion of indebtedness to constraints from Cocks (1989: 29). Resentment and overcoming are two of Nietzsche's favourite themes.

3. The following section deals with an interpretive problem involved in treating Foucault's writing as a unified oeuvre. It can be skipped without adversely affecting the reader's grasp of the book.

4. There are several introductory volumes that offer exegeses of Foucault's main texts. Shumway (1992) is probably most accessible for the student approaching Foucault from the concerns of the humanities, tending to focus more on Foucault's earlier work. Bernauer (1990) provides an inclusive philosophical account of the development of Foucault's thought through four stages, drawing on many of his minor texts and interviews. For sociologists, Smart (1988) offers an excellent brief overview. Other general reviews have become dated because they do not cover Foucault's later work.

5. Some commentators have no hesitation in interpreting Foucault as they would any other author, attempting to establish the final meaning of his work. See, for example, Bird (1989: 85–6) and Walzer (1989: 193). Gane (1986: 111) depicts interpretations of Foucault written after his death as a kind of post-mortem conducted by those for whom Foucault 'requires to be pinned down and examined'.

6. Gillan (1988: 34) admonishes that any interpretation of Foucault's writing must not bypass Foucault's own rules for the analysis of discourse, ruling out reference to author, oeuvre or fundamental intention as the basis of unity.

7. See 1980f: 115; 1982a: 208; 1984b: 351–2; 1988s: 257–8.

8. See 1972a: 14–15; 1980j: 184; 1988p: 19; 1988s: 255–6.

9. For example, whereas Dews (1989) attributes Foucault's turn to subjectivity in his later work to the earlier dilemmas that remain unresolved, Bernauer (1990) sees it as a stage in the coherent evolution of Foucault's thought. For Dews, Foucault's work is constrained by its initial errors, while for Bernauer it unfolds its initial promise over time.

10. The French biography by Eribon (1991) contains details of Foucault's earlier life and influences, as well as his political activities. James Miller (1993) describes his book not as a biography but as a narrative account of Foucault's struggle to become what he was. He therefore focuses on Foucault's life, in particular his experiments with gay and sadomasochistic subcultures in the USA. His book attempts to offer an interpretive key to Foucault's philosophy by explaining it in terms of transgressive limit experiences that culminated in death. Miller conflates Foucault's middle course of work on limits with the urge to escape all limits, thereby producing a one-sided but intriguing interpretation of Foucault, especially of the intellectual and personal influences that pulled Foucault to the pole of limitless transgression.

11. See 1965: 269–78; 1973a; 1975a; 1980g; 1980m; and 1988d.

12. Foucault writes of a well-prepared suicide as 'the simplest of pleasures' (1979g).

13. He makes this claim in 1988i: 11; and 1988l: 6. To be exact, the book he wrote is *Folie et Déraison* (1961), reissued as *Histoire de la Folie* (1972b). *Madness and Civilization* is a translation of an abridged version.

14. The publications I refer to here include a commentary on the work of Binswanger (1984–5), and an attempt to explain mental illness (1954). Although Foucault significantly revised the latter in a version also available in English translation (1987c), he excluded it from what he considered his work (Eribon 1991: 70).

15. For examples, see 1963; 1977a, b, c, d, e, f; 1983c; 1987a; and 1990a.

16. See 1981g; 1985a; 1988j; and 1993.

17. See 1979b; 1981c, d, f; 1988k; Burchell 1991; and Gordon 1991.

18. Foucault discussed gay issues in interviews. See 1980n; 1982b; 1983b; 1984h; and 1989d.

2 Foucault's Critical Ethos

1. Foucault treats Kant's text substantially in his own reply to the question 'What is Enlightenment?' (1984c) and also in 'Kant on Enlightenment and Revolution' (1986b). Yet the theme crops up in other pieces too, suggesting that it had more than a passing significance for Foucault's work. See 1980l: 52–4; 1982a: 215–16; and 1983a: 199. See Gordon (1986) for his discussion of the same theme.

2. Foucault translated and commented on Kant's *Anthropology from a Pragmatic*

Point of View as part of the requirements for his doctorate. Kant's book, which is usually ignored, answers the question of what Man is by offering maxims and homilies about human behaviour (J. Miller, 1993: 139–40).

3. The question of whether Foucault interprets Kant correctly remains open. Schnädelbach (1992) argues that Foucault's characterization of modern thought applies only to left Hegelianism and phenomenology. Moreover, Kant's philosophy is concerned with the finitude of human knowledge, not Man as a finite being, so that Kant's thought is not anthropological in the way that Foucault suggests. The human being is merely the site at which rational science and morality are actualized.

4. See Bernauer (1990: 202, note 133), for the relevant reference in Kant.

5. As Gordon (1980: 241–2) notes, the critical demand to analyse the particular rationality of the present, its effects and conditions runs counter to rationalist historicism. Rather than assuming the perpetual progress of rationalization, Foucault undertakes a 'history of the present' which regards the present as a singular event of rationality rather than an episode in a series of progressions.

3 The Analysis of Limits

1. Dreyfus and Rabinow (1982: 45–8) elucidate what Foucault meant by statement in comparison with the concept of speech act, concluding that it can be understood as a serious speech act with scientific and veridical significance. I have not attempted here to provide a full account of Foucault's archaeological method. See Dreyfus and Rabinow (1982: 44–103), Gutting (1989), Major-Poetzl (1983), d'Amico (1989: 73–107), Deleuze (1988: 1–22), Hacking (1986), and Megill (1985: 202–32) for commentaries and critiques of archaeology.

2. Although *The Order of Things* is often regarded as Foucault's masterpiece, it is, to say the least, somewhat esoteric, being aimed at specialists in the history of science (1989b: 99). Great familiarity with its contents is thus not necessary for an assessment of Foucault as a political thinker. Readers interested in learning more but daunted by the book itself might find it useful to consult the relevant chapters of Gutting (1989), Major-Poetzl (1983) and Shumway (1992). Dreyfus and Rabinow (1982: 16–43) discuss the start of the book and the section about the analytic of finitude that I address below.

3. For Foucault's graphic systematization of the arrangements of the three epistemes, see 1973b: 201.

4. This historical rather than epistemological approach to truth is what Rajchman (1985: 51) calls Foucault's 'historical nominalism'.

5. See 1982a: 208; 1984b: 351; 1984d: 336–9; 1984f: 386–7; 1987b: 4.

6. Foucault claimed retrospectively that he had looked at delinquency primarily from the perspective of power, in *Discipline and Punish*; at medicine primarily from the perspective of truth in *Birth of the Clinic*, while *The Order of*

Things also focused on truth; at sexuality primarily as an ethics in *The History of Sexuality*. He was in two minds about whether he had focused on truth in his study of madness and psychiatry or whether *Madness and Civilization* confused all three axes (1984b: 352; 1984d: 336–8; 1984f: 386–7).

7. P. Miller (1987) suggests that Foucault views power as the promotion of subjectivity via regulatory practices of the self, or as 'a multiplicity of practices for the promotion and regulation of subjectivity' (10), noting that by doing so Foucault reverses the prevailing view of power as repression of essential subjectivity, and suggesting that we replace Foucault's term 'power' with 'regulatory practices of the self' (17). Commentary on and critique of Foucault's notion of power has become an intellectual industry in itself. For an incomplete list, see Balbus, 1986; Bird, 1989; Cocks, 1989; Dallmayr, 1984; Deleuze, 1988; Dreyfus and Rabinow, 1982; Fraser, 1981; Hartsock, 1990; Hendley, 1988; Hiley, 1984; Hoy, 1986b; Ingram, 1986; Keenan, 1987; Lemert and Gillan, 1982; Megill, 1985; Minson, 1986; Patton, 1989; Philp, 1983; Poulantzas, 1978; Said, 1986; Schneck, 1987; Sheridan, 1980; Smart, 1988; Taylor, 1984, 1985, 1989; Walzer, 1989; West, 1987; Wickham, 1986.

8. The term 'other' signifies radical alterity in the form of a person or attribute of humanity which we are unable to understand or to be reconciled with.

9. Note how Foucault's concept of ethics differs from conventional notions, which focus on the relation between oneself and others.

10. 'Will to Knowledge' would be the translation of the French subtitle of the first volume of *The History of Sexuality*. It is clearly an echo of Nietzsche's (1966: 9) phrase 'the will to truth'.

11. Gordon (1991: 4) also suggests that Foucault's macro-analysis of government was a response to criticisms of his work which claimed that his micro-analysis ignored global political questions, especially relations between state and society.

12. Miller and Rose (1992) use the term 'translation' to characterize the instantiation of government through the assemblage of mechanisms and techniques. My terminology is slightly different from theirs in that they regard political programmes as translations of rationalities, whereas I distinguish between the rationalities of micro- and macro-programmes.

13. Even though Foucault distinguishes between police as utopian plans, institutional rules and academic discipline (1988k: 154), and is aware that mercantilism was a failure (1979b: 15), his account of police tends to give the impression of an effectiveness that is not historically justified. This should not dull us to the greater potential of contemporary policing embodied in the apparatus of the state and to the forms of individualization linked to it (1982a: 216).

14. Burchell (1991) and Gordon (1991) draw on unpublished lectures presented by Foucault at the Collège de France in 1978 and 1979. I rely on their accounts here and in later reviews of Foucault's discussions about liberalism.

15. See Rose, 1990.

4 The Limits of Humanism

1. Sheridan's (1980) overview of Foucault's major works up to 1980 gives the reader a good flavour of Foucault's texts by citing extensively from them.

2. Foucault is referring to Nietzsche (1966: 9).

3. Mill's (1975) essay *On Liberty* is a clear case for freedom as a condition of possibility of truth.

4. As we shall see, this is the logic of Taylor's criticism of Foucault (Taylor, 1984, 1985).

5. Foucault himself does not make the two meanings of subject clear when he defines them as 'subject to someone else by control . . . and tied to his own identity by a conscience' (1982a: 212). He does not give us two meanings of the word 'subject', but two senses of *assujettir*, which can mean to fix or fasten as well as to subjugate or subject.

5 Foucault's Regicide of Political Philosophy

1. This is the sort of legitimation invoked by communitarians such as Taylor (1991).

2. Recently Shapiro (1990) has attempted to construct such a political theory. In general, political theories that argue from the basis of the place of human nature in the natural order and its realization through politics are termed Aristotelian (Plant, 1991: 23–4). Other political philosophies, notably those of Hobbes, Locke and Rousseau, claim to tell the truth about human nature as revealed in a 'state of nature'.

3. Among other such procedures, Habermas (1979: 205) cites Rawls's original position, but his own project is to elaborate 'the normative content of the universal presuppositions of communication' as a regulative ideal for society.

4. For alternative definitions along similar lines that stress extra-political foundations, see Nelson (1986: 158), and Ripstein (1987: 115).

5. Honig (1993) analyses the exclusions at work in the political theory of a leading communitarian, Michael Sandel. My discussions below of Taylor and Walzer invoke the same spirit as her book, which argues that 'Most political theorists are hostile to the disruptions of politics.' She asks whether the efforts to confine political contest to tasks of adjudication, regulation and consensus building do not 'harbor dangers and violences of their own' (2). Such theorists occlude the political practices by which subjects are made to fit their social and political identities while denying that these practices are responsible for the resistance they provoke whenever identities do not fit (3).

6. On occasion Foucault (1974: 160) endorses the view that common law is bourgeois political law, leading him to urge working-class solidarity, including its delinquent fringe, against the exercise of bourgeois power through the law. However, he also condemns forms of socialism (such as Blanquism) that

conceive of class struggle in terms that require the elimination of the class enemy (1991: 60–1).

7. There might seem to be some similarity between Foucault's concept of thought here and a whole discourse emphasizing human consciousness as what makes our behaviour meaningful and peculiarly human. Clearly his formulation is incompatible with any structuralist or determinist account which treats consciousness as ephemeral. Foucault, however, does not posit thought as the bearer of meaning, the expression of the original Idea that justifies human existence. He does not refer to thought in the sense of a *cogito* which is equated with our existence. Rather, thought is one element of our experience, albeit one of strategic importance for freedom. In fact, Foucault's formulation is much closer to contemporary notions of the integration of thought and action which also revive the concept of praxis. See Bernstein (1972).

8. Gordon (1987: 298) remarks that this is a 'field of historical data. . . which . . . although it has certainly not been unknown to previous scholarship, has seldom been accorded . . . adequate appraisal'.

9. Foucault is referring to liberalism in a broad sense according to the European tradition, rather than in the American sense as that which is contrasted with conservatism. My own usage of the term is intended to include political theories ranging from social democracy to monetarism and conservatism.

10. The phrase 'actually existing liberalism' is an echo of Bahro's (1978) 'actually existing socialism'.

11. Foucault's detailed comments on liberalism have not been published, so I have relied on Gordon's (1991) and Burchell's (1991) accounts of his lectures.

12. Elsewhere Foucault mistakenly suggests that a social contract is the only liberal solution to the problem of demonstrating social cohesion (1981d: 357).

13. Gordon (1991: 46–7) suggests that Foucault was intrigued by the social market of the *Ordoliberalen* as a game of freedom sustained by government intervention. I take it that his attraction was to their self-reflectivity concerning the conditions of possibility for that game rather than the game itself.

14. The constitution of the entrepreneurial self has been analysed in detail by Rose (1990).

15 An extreme example of this inner freedom appears in Victor Frankl's (1962) *Man's Search for Meaning*, where it is claimed that even in a concentration camp one is free to choose one's own attitude.

16. For examples of critiques that do not recognize the limits of the truths they tell (about the needs of children), see Balbus (1986) and Horowitz (1987). Other critics who argue that Foucault must have access to some form of truth if his criticism is to be valid include Fraser (1981), Habermas (1987), Hartsock (1990) and Megill (1985). In contrast, Gutting (1989), Keenan (1987), Paden (1987) and Schneck (1987) all suggest ways in which Foucault's arguments can stand without his privileging the veracity of his own statements over those of others.

17. Other critics who insist that Foucault's philosophy requires principles or normative criteria include Fraser (1981, 1985); Habermas (1987); Paternek (1987). They all conclude that Foucault implicitly appeals to or presupposes humanist, liberal values. These opinions indicate the persistence of the parameters of political philosophy, in their insistence on normative grounding.

18. Both Hooke (1987) and Moore (1987) perceive an ethical stance in Foucault's work that is overlooked by critics. However, their defence underplays Foucault's departure from humanist ethics.

19. Philp (1983) also argues that Foucault's radical critique is incoherent in the absence of a vision of a better future. Hiley (1984) claims that Foucault's work is devoid of the hope requested by another anti-foundationalist philosopher, Richard Rorty.

20. Other critics do hold to notions of essential, natural or autonomous subjectivity as the grounds of political philosophy. See Balbus (1986), Horowitz (1987), and West (1987). Philp (1983) argues that there is a naturalistic anthropology underlying Foucault's work that remains unelaborated. Less hostile commentators also detect thin conceptions of the subject that underwrite capacities of resistance and guide Foucault's ideas about ethical self-formation. See Moore (1987), Patton (1989), and Schneck (1987). On the other hand, Wapner (1989) argues that what is most disconcerting about Foucault's political project is that it does not rest on a notion of the human subject. White (1986) offers the most cogent critique in this regard, as he identifies the excluded 'other' in Foucault's work with an aesthetic subject. Foucault's attraction to the realm of aesthetic creation as a possible realm of unlimited freedom makes White's identification plausible, but not incontrovertible.

21. There is another limit or ground that is appealed to in humanist political philosophy, that of the aesthetic. Later this ground will be described as a pole of limitless freedom to which Foucault is attracted as an escape from the unbearable constraint of humanism.

22. There is a broadly communitarian argument that only a society in which there was already implicit consensus about such wrongs would resist them, no matter how much political philosophy there was. See Plant (1991: 345–50).

6 Transgression and Aesthetics

1. Foucault's study of Raymond Roussel (1987a) is an extended analysis of one author working on the limits of foundationless language by inventing language games.

2. In contrast, Rajchman (1985) perceives a shift in Foucault's work when he abandons his faith in the transgressive force of avant-garde literature as the expression of experiences excluded by modernity, such as madness and eroticism. Rajchman's interpretation seems to rest on an unnecessary but not unjustified identification of artistic transgression with transcendence of all limits.

3. Foucault severely criticized the notion that literature itself was either autonomous or in itself subversive (1988a: 309).

4. Foucault (1988o: 87–94) ascribes these changes in ethics to new political conditions involved in the change from the relatively certain politics of the city to the precarious position of even privileged citizens in the empire.

5. Foucault undermines the distinction he draws between Greek and Hellenist ethics by arguing that the latter 'are at the same time universally valid principles and rules for those who wish to give their existence an honorable and noble form. It is the lawless universality of an aesthetics of existence that in any case is practised only by a few' (1988o: 184–5).

6. According to Foucault (1987b: 243–4) the path to self-formation according to knowledge rather than art was opened by Platonic erotics, which took the first steps into an enquiry into desiring Man.

7. Deleuze (1988: 100) hits the nail on the head in that he sees that Foucault's interest is in the detachment of the relation to oneself from power and knowledge, but I do not accept Deleuze's case that Foucault presents an account of such completely differentiated ethics.

8. Foucault's analysis of Christianity is fragmentary because the projected fourth volume of *The History of Sexuality*, to be entitled *The Confessions of the Flesh* (1987b: 12), was not ready for publication by the time Foucault died.

9. In both 1988k and 1993 Foucault distinguishes quite sharply between bodily enacted penitence in early Christianity and verbalized confession in the fourth century.

10. Burckhardt (1935: 160) discusses fame being achieved in the Renaissance by courtiers who made their lives models of moderation and harmony. Foucault sees in this an example of 'the hero as his own work of art' (1984b: 370).

11. Nietzsche's attitude may well have provided Foucault with the motivation to write the second and third volumes of *The History of Sexuality*. He claims that his interest in the notion of style, and hence the stylization of conduct, is derived from Peter Brown's work (1988r: 244–5), but perhaps Nietzsche provided the impetus for that interest.

12. Several commentators do not distinguish sufficiently between Foucault's critiques of humanist assumptions about the existence of the subject and his interest in promoting new subjectivities. They argue that the 'turn to the subject' in Foucault's later work indicates that his earlier work lacked the ground of a notion of subjectivity. See for example Dews (1989).

13. Eagleton (1990) argues that the discourse about art, i.e. aesthetics, has been central to modern political thought because it provides ideological representations of self-regulating autonomy which compensate for the absence of such community in capitalist societies.

14. As we shall see, this is the sort of analysis proposed by Habermas (1984), which underlies several critiques of Foucault as an aestheticist.

7 Theoretical Transgression of Limits

1. This position is not as opposed as it might first appear to Foucault's earlier proclamation that '"The whole of society" is precisely that which should not be considered except as something to be destroyed' (1977i: 233). 'The whole of society' refers to a totalitarian utopian conception that conceals concrete operations of power.

2. As we shall see, though, Foucault was unhappy about gay identity politics that grounds itself in such claims and thereby reinforces the general deployment of sexuality and its normalizing discourses.

3. Foucault does not need to demonstrate that resistances do become winning strategies in order to defend his claim that resistance is always possible, as there is a difference between success and possibility. Scott (1990) suggests that there is much subtle recalcitrance, even in oppressive social structures, which is not even noticed by those who dominate, yet may become the background for open resistance. As similar sabotage and guileful unruliness occurs in slavery, it should also be considered a power relationship, contrary to Foucault's opinion.

4. See the footnote by Leslie Sawyer in 1982a: 222.

5. See 1988f for Foucault's discussion of the Iranian revolution.

6. One might argue that the comparison is misplaced as, among other differences, the Jews of the Warsaw ghetto could expect to die whether they resisted or not. However, they certainly refused to obey and comply with the Nazi death machine, unlike many of their fellow Jews.

7. James Miller (1993: 177, 308) notes that Foucault had also been impressed by the same willingness for sacrifice during his experience of insurrection in Tunisia.

8. Foucault discusses Magritte's interest in such *heterotopias* (1983c: 4).

9. Foucault does not appear to have considered that his own efforts to create a space for prisoners to speak for themselves contributed to this development (Eribon, 1989: 248).

8 Practical Transgression of Limits

1. Given the current religious right campaign against education about 'alternative lifestyles' in American schools, one might question whether the stage of appealing to naturalism is over. In order to counter allegations that such education seduces students into experimenting with gay and lesbian sexuality, it is argued by some gay activists that one either is or is not homosexual.

2. For an analysis of sadomasochism as a perversion that was constructed according to scientific discourses in the late nineteenth century along with homosexuality, and sexuality in general, see Davidson (1990: 120–32).

3. Indeed, there are striking parallels between the dynamics of relations between

gay and lesbian and S/M subcultures, including 'a second "coming out"' (Thompson, 1991: 169), blaming the spread of AIDS on sadomasochists (136), or a general sense of abhorrence.

4. My main sources for accounts of S/M are Thompson (1991), which deals mostly with gay but also some lesbian and even heterosexual S/M, and Samois (1987), which deals with lesbian S/M. J. Miller (1993: 259–69) also provides an introduction to the topic.

5. There are other grounds for feminist critiques of S/M as presented by its 'libertarian' feminist practitioners. When it is argued that S/M is about the liberation of repressed sexuality, or that it is valid because it is contractual and consensual, it can be criticized on Foucauldian grounds (Diamond and Quinby, 1988: 199–200; Sawicki, 1988: 182).

6. In the contemporary West an enormous range of such technologies is in circulation, ranging from twelve-step 'recovery' programmes to Zen Buddhism, in addition to the ingrained social technologies of family, welfare agencies, educational institutions and organized religion.

7. I argue in Chapter 6 that Foucault overlooks the cultural arrangements of the West that constitute conditions of possibility for modernist aesthetic protest.

9 Foucault in Contemporary Political Theory

1. Woodhull (1988: 170–1) points out that Foucault's suggestion to decriminalize rape is incompatible with desexualization because it overlooks the links between sex and power by treating rape as a crime of power.

2. Fraser (1985: 181–2) suggests that a posthumanist ethic that moves beyond the problem of humanist autonomy might be elaborated within American feminism.

3. In Chapter 5 I argue that communitarianism and liberal pluralism, exemplified by Taylor and Walzer respectively, both tend toward closure. Connolly (1991a) and Honig (1993) also offer criticisms of liberal and communitarian theories that stress their similar strategies for foreclosing political issues.

4. I allude to the three paths of invention, discovery and interpretation which Walzer (1987) argues are available for political theory. From the perspective of aesthetics of political existence, the distinctions between the three paths are less significant than their similarities.

Bibliography

Works by Michel Foucault

Dates of original publication (usually in French), and of interviews and lectures, are given in square brackets where they differ from the citation date, in order to indicate the chronological sequence of Foucault's work.

1954. *Maladie Mentale et Personnalité*. Paris: Presses Universitaires de France.

1961. *Folie et Déraison: Histoire de la Folie à l'Age Classique*. Paris: Plon.

1962. *Maladie Mentale et Psychologie*. Paris: Presse Universitaires de France.

1963. 'Distance, Aspect, Origine'. *Critique* 19(198) (November): 931–45.

1965 [1961]. *Madness and Civilization*. Trans. Richard Howard. New York: Pantheon.

1971a. 'A Conversation with Michel Foucault'. Interview. *Partisan Review* 38: 192–201.

1971b. 'Monstrosities in Criticism.'. Trans. Robert J. Matthews. *Diacritics* 1(1) (Fall): 57–60.

1972a [1969]. *The Archaeology of Knowledge*. Trans. Alan Sheridan. New York: Pantheon.

1972b [1961]. *Histoire de la Folie à l'Age Classique*. Paris: Gallimard.

1973a [1963]. *The Birth of the Clinic: An Archaeology of Medical Perception*. Trans. Alan Sheridan. London: Tavistock.

1973b [1966]. *The Order of Things: An Archaeology of the Human Sciences*. Trans. unidentified collective. New York: Vintage.

1974 [1972]. 'Michel Foucault on Attica: An Interview'. Trans. John K. Simon. *Telos* 19 (Spring): 154–61.

1975a [1973]. 'Foreword'. Trans. Frank Jellinek. In *I, Pierre Rivière, Having Slaughtered My Mother, My Sister and My Brother: A Case of Parricide in the 19th Century*, ed. Michel Foucault. New York: Pantheon.

1975b [1973]. 'Tales of Murder'. Trans. Frank Jellinek. *I, Pierre Rivière, Having Slaughtered My Mother, My Sister, and My Brother: A Case of Parricide in the 19th Century*, ed. Michel Foucault. New York: Pantheon.

1976 [1976]. 'The Politics of Crime'. Trans. Mollie Horwitz. *Partisan Review* 43(3): 453–9.

1977a [1962]. 'The Father's "No"'. In *Language, Counter-Memory, Practice: Selected Essays and Interviews*, trans. Donald Bouchard and Sherry Simon, ed. Donald Bouchard. Ithaca: Cornell University Press.

1977b [1963]. 'A Preface to Transgression'. In *Language, Counter-Memory, Practice: Selected Essays and Interviews*, trans. Donald Bouchard and Sherry Simon, ed. Donald Bouchard. Ithaca: Cornell University Press.

1977c [1963]. 'Language to Infinity'. In *Language, Counter-Memory, Practice: Selected Essays and Interviews*, trans. Donald Bouchard and Sherry Simon, ed. Donald Bouchard. Ithaca: Cornell University Press.

1977d [1964]. 'Fantasia of the Library'. In *Language, Counter-Memory, Practice: Selected Essays and Interviews*, trans. Donald Bouchard and Sherry Simon, ed. Donald Bouchard. Ithaca: Cornell University Press.

1977e [1969]. 'What is an Author?' In *Language, Counter-Memory, Practice: Selected Essays and Interviews*, trans. Donald Bouchard, and Sherry Simon & ed. Donald Bouchard. Ithaca: Cornell University Press.

1977f [1970]. 'Theatricum Philosophicum.' In *Language, Counter-Memory, Practice: Selected Essays and Interviews*, trans. Donald Bouchard, and Sherry Simon & ed. Donald Bouchard. Ithaca: Cornell University Press.

1977g [1971]. 'History of Systems of Thought.' In *Language, Counter-Memory, Practice: Selected Essays and Interviews*, trans. Donald Bouchard and Sherry Simon, ed. Donald Bouchard. Ithaca: Cornell University Press.

1977h [1972]. 'Intellectuals and Power'. In *Language, Counter-Memory, Practice: Selected Essays and Interviews*, trans. Donald Bouchard and Sherry Simon, ed. Donald Bouchard. Ithaca: Cornell University Press.

1977i [1973]. 'Revolutionary Action: Until Now'. In *Language, Counter-Memory, Practice: Selected Essays and Interviews*, trans. Donald Bouchard and Sherry Simon, ed. Donald Bouchard. Ithaca: Cornell University Press.

1977j [1977]. 'The Political Function of the Intellectual'. Trans. Colin Gordon. *Radical Philosophy* 17 (Summer): 12–14.

1977k [1977]. 'Power and Sex: An Interview with Michel Foucault'. Trans. David J. Parent. *Telos* 32 (Summer): 152–61.

1977l [1972]. 'Preface'. In *Anti-Oedipus: Capitalism and Schizophrenia*, by Gilles Deleuze and Felix Guattari. New York: Viking Press.

1978a [1968]. 'Politics and the Study of Discourse'. Trans. Colin Gordon. *Ideology and Consciousness* 4 (Autumn): 7–26.

1978b [1976]. *The History of Sexuality: An Introduction*. Trans. Robert Hurley. Harmondsworth: Penguin.

1978c [1966]. 'Interview with Michel Foucault.' Interview. In *Les Livres Des Autres*, ed. Raymond Bellour. Paris: Union Generale d'Editions.

1978d [1967]. 'Second Interview with Michel Foucault.' Interview. In *Les Livres Des Autres*, ed. Raymond Bellour. Paris: Union Generale d'Editions.

1978e [1976]. 'The West and the Truth of Sex'. Trans. Lawrence E. Winters. *Sub-Stance*, no. 20: 5–8.

1978f [1977]. 'La Grande Colère des Faits'. In *Faut-il Brûler les Nouveaux Philosophes?*, ed. Sylvie Bouscasse and Denis Bourgeois. Paris: Nouvelles Editions Oswald.

1979a [1975]. *Discipline and Punish: The Birth of the Prison*. Trans. Alan Sheridan. New York: Vintage.

1979b [1978]. 'Governmentality'. Trans. Rosi Braidotti. *Ideology and Consciousness* 6 (Autumn): 5–21.

1979c [1976]. 'War in the Filigree of Peace: Course Summary'. Trans. Ian Mcleod. *Oxford Literary Review* 4(2) (Autumn): 15–19.

1979d [1971]. 'My Body, This Paper, This Fire'. Trans. Geoff Bennington. *Oxford Literary Review* 4(1) (August): 9–28.

1979e [1976]. 'Power and Norm: Notes'. Trans. W. Suchting. In *Michel Foucault: Power, Truth, Strategy*, ed. Meaghan Morris and Paul Patton. Sydney: Feral Publications.

1979f [1977]. 'The Life of Infamous Men'. Trans. Paul Foss, and Meaghan Morris. In *Michel Foucault: Power, Truth, Strategy*, ed. Meaghan Morris and Paul Patton. Sydney: Feral Publications.

1979g. 'The Simplest of Pleasures'. Trans. Mike Riegle and Gilles Barbedette. *Fag Rag*, no. 29: 3.

1980a [1972]. 'On Popular Justice: A Discussion with Maoists'. Trans. John Mepham. In *Power/Knowledge: Selected Interviews and Other Writings, 1972–1977*, ed. Colin Gordon. Brighton: Harvester.

1980b [1975]. 'Prison Talk'. Trans. Colin Gordon. In *Power/Knowledge: Selected Interviews and Other Writings, 1972–1977*, ed. Colin Gordon. Brighton: Harvester.

1980c [1975]. 'Body/Power'. Trans. Colin Gordon. In *Power/Knowledge: Selected Interviews and Other Writings, 1972–1977*, ed. Colin Gordon. Brighton: Harvester.

1980d [1976]. 'Questions on Geography'. Trans. Colin Gordon. In *Power/Knowledge: Selected Interviews and Other Writings, 1972–1977*, ed. Colin Gordon. Brighton: Harvester.

1980e [1976]. 'Two Lectures'. Trans. Kate Soper. In *Power/Knowledge: Selected Interviews and Other Writings, 1972–1977*, ed. Colin Gordon. Brighton: Harvester.

1980f [1976]. 'Truth and Power'. Trans. Colin Gordon. In *Power/Knowledge: Selected Interviews and Other Writings, 1972–1977*, ed. Colin Gordon. Brighton: Harvester.

1980g [1976]. 'The Politics of Health in the Eighteenth Century'. Trans. Colin Gordon. In *Power/Knowledge: Selected Interviews and Other Writings, 1972–1977*, ed. Colin Gordon. Brighton: Harvester.

1980h [1977]. 'Powers and Strategies'. Trans. Colin Gordon. In *Power/Knowledge: Selected Interviews and Other Writings, 1972–1977*, ed. Colin Gordon. Brighton: Harvester.

1980i [1977]. 'The Eye of Power'. Trans. Colin Gordon. In *Power/Knowledge: Selected Interviews and Other Writings, 1972–1977*, ed. Colin Gordon. Brighton: Harvester.

1980j [1977]. 'The History of Sexuality'. Trans. Leo Marshall. In *Power/Knowledge: Selected Interviews and Other Writings, 1972–1977*, ed. Colin Gordon. Brighton: Harvester.

1980k [1977]. 'The Confession of the Flesh'. In *Power/Knowledge: Selected Interviews and Other Writings, 1972–1977*, ed. Colin Gordon. Brighton: Harvester.

1980l [1978]. 'Georges Canguilhem: Philosopher of Error'. Trans. Graham Burchell.

I & C 7 (Autumn): 51–62.

1980m. 'Introduction'. *Herculine Barbin: Being the Recently Discovered Memoirs of a Nineteenth Century Hermaphrodite*. Trans. Richard McDougal. New York: Pantheon.

1980n. 'Conversation with Michel Foucault'. Interview. *The Threepenny Review* 1(1) (Winter–Spring): 4–5.

1980o. 'La Poussière et le Nuage.' In *L'Impossible Prison*, ed. Michelle Perrot. Paris: Éditions du Seuil.

1981a [1970]. 'The Order of Discourse'. Trans. Ian McLeod. In *Untying the Text*, ed. Robert Young. London: Routledge & Kegan Paul.

1981b [1978]. 'Questions of Method: An Interview with Michel Foucault'. Trans. Colin Gordon. *I & C* 8 (Spring): 3–14.

1981c [1978]. 'Foucault at the Collège de France I: A Course Summary'. Trans. James Bernauer. *Philosophy and Social Criticism* 8(2) (Summer): 235–42.

1981d [1979]. 'Foucault at the Collège de France II: A Course Summary'. Trans. James Bernauer. *Philosophy and Social Criticism* 8(3) (Fall): 349–59.

1981e [1979]. 'Is It Useless to Revolt?' Trans. James Bernauer. *Philosophy and Social Criticism* 8(1) (Spring): 5–9.

1981f [1979]. 'Omnes et Singulatim'. In *The Tanner Lectures on Human Values II*, ed. Sterling McCurrin. Salt Lake City: University of Utah Press.

1981g. 'Sexuality and Solitude'. *London Review of Books* (21 May - 3 June).

1982a. 'The Subject and Power'. Afterword to *Michel Foucault: Beyond Structuralism and Hermeneutics*, by Hubert L. Dreyfus and Paul Rabinow. Brighton: Harvester Press.

1982b. 'The Social Triumph of the Sexual Will'. Interview. Trans. Brendan Lemon. *Christopher Street*, no. 64 (May): 36–41.

1982c. '19th Century Imaginations'. Trans. Alex Susteric. *Semiotext(e)* 4(2): 182–90.

1983a. 'Structuralism and Post-Structuralism: An Interview with Michel Foucault by Gerard Raulet'. Trans. Jeremy Harding. *Telos 55* (Spring): 195–211.

1983b [1982]. 'Sexual Choice, Sexual Act: An Interview with Michel Foucault'. Trans. James O'Higgins. *Salmagundi 58/59* (Fall 1982/ Winter 1983): 10–24.

1983c [1973]. *This Is Not a Pipe*. Trans. James Harkness. Berkeley: University of California Press.

1983d. 'Discourse and Truth: The Problematization of Parrhesia'. Notes to the seminar given by Foucault at the University of California at Berkeley, edited by Joseph Pearson.

1983e. 'La Pologne, et après?' Interview. *Le Débat*, no. 25 (May): 3–34.

1984–85 [1954]. 'Dream, Imagination, and Existence'. Trans. Forrest Williams. *Review of Existential Psychology & Psychiatry* 19(1): 31–78.

1984a [1971]. 'Nietzsche, Genealogy, History'. Trans. Donald Bouchard and Sherry Simon. In *The Foucault Reader*, ed. Paul Rabinow. New York: Pantheon.

1984b [1983]. 'On the Genealogy of Ethics: An Overview of Work in Progress'. In *The Foucault Reader*, ed. Paul Rabinow. New York: Pantheon.

1984c. 'What is Enlightenment?' Trans. Catherine Porter. In *The Foucault Reader*, ed. Paul Rabinow. New York: Pantheon.

1984d. 'Preface to *The History of Sexuality, Vol. 2*'. In *The Foucault Reader*, ed. Paul Rabinow. New York: Pantheon.

1984e. 'Politics and Ethics: An Interview'. Trans. Catherine Porter. In *The Foucault Reader*, ed. Paul Rabinow. New York: Pantheon.

1984f. 'Polemics, Politics and Problemizations'. Trans. Lydia Davis. In *The Foucault Reader*, ed. Paul Rabinow. New York: Pantheon.

1984g [1982]. 'Space, Knowledge, and Power'. Trans. Christian Hubert. In *The Foucault Reader*, ed. Paul Rabinow. New York: Pantheon.

1984h. 'Sex, Power and the Politics of Identity.' Interview. *The Advocate*, no. 400 (7 August): 26–30, 58.

1984i [1981]. 'Face Aux Gouvernements, les Droits de l'Homme'. *Libération* (30 June – 1 July): 22.

1985a [1983]. 'The Battle for Chastity'. In *Western Sexuality: Practice and Precept in Past and Present Times*, trans. Anthony Forster, ed. Philippe Aries and Andre Bejin. Oxford: Basil Blackwell.

1985b [1975]. 'An Interview with Michel Foucault'. Trans. Renee Morel. *History of the Present* 1 (February): 2–3, 14.

1986a [1967]. 'Nietzsche, Freud, Marx'. Trans. Jon Anderson and Gary Hentzi. *Critical Texts* 3(2) (Winter): 1–5.

1986b [1983]. 'Kant on Enlightenment and Revolution'. Trans. Colin Gordon. *Economy and Society* 15(1) (February): 88–96.

1986c. *Sept Propos sur le Septième Ange*. Montpellier: Editions Fata Morgana.

1986d [1984/1967]. 'Of Other Spaces'. Trans. Jay Miskowiec. *Diacritics* 16(1) (Spring): 22–7.

1987a [1963]. *Death and the Labyrinth: The World of Raymond Roussel*. Trans. Charles Ruas. Berkeley: University of California Press.

1987b [1984]. *The Use of Pleasure: The History of Sexuality, Volume 2*. Trans. Robert Hurley. Harmondsworth: Penguin.

1987c [1962]. *Mental Illness and Psychology*. Trans. Alan Sheridan. Berkeley: University of California Press.

1988a [1975]. 'The Functions of Literature'. In *Politics, Philosophy, Culture: Interviews and Other Writings, 1977–1984*, trans. Alan Sheridan et al., ed. Lawrence D. Kritzman. New York: Routledge.

1988b [1977]. 'Confinement, Psychiatry, Prison'. In *Politics, Philosophy, Culture: Interviews and Other Writings, 1977–1984*, trans. Alan Sheridan et al., ed. Lawrence D. Kritzman. New York: Routledge.

1988c [1978]. 'On Power'. In *Politics, Philosophy, Culture: Interviews and Other Writings, 1977–1984*, trans. Alan Sheridan, and others & ed. Lawrence D. Kritzman. New York: Routledge.

1988d [1978]. 'The Dangerous Individual.' In *Politics, Philosophy, Culture: Interviews and Other Writings, 1977-1984*, trans. Alan Sheridan, and others & ed. Lawrence D. Kritzman. New York: Routledge.

1988e [1978]. 'Sexual Morality and the Law'. In *Politics, Philosophy, Culture: Interviews and Other Writings, 1977-1984*, trans. Alan Sheridan et al., ed. Lawrence D. Kritzman. New York: Routledge.

1988f [1979]. 'Iran: The Spirit of a World Without Spirit'. In *Politics, Philosophy, Culture: Interviews and Other Writings, 1977–1984*, trans. Alan Sheridan et al., ed. Lawrence D. Kritzman. New York: Routledge.

1988g [1980]. 'The Masked Philosopher'. In *Politics, Philosophy, Culture: Interviews and Other Writings, 1977–1984*, trans. Alan Sheridan et al., ed.

Lawrence D. Kritzman. New York: Routledge.

1988h [1981]. 'Practicing Criticism'. In *Politics, Philosophy, Culture: Interviews and Other Writings, 1977–1984*, trans. Alan Sheridan et al., ed. Lawrence D. Kritzman. New York: Routledge.

1988i [1982]. 'Truth, Power, Self: An Interview with Michel Foucault'. In *Technologies of the Self: A Seminar with Michel Foucault*, ed. Luther H. Martin, Huck Gutman and Patrick H. Hutton. London: Tavistock.

1988j [1982]. 'Technologies of the Self'. In *Technologies of the Self: A Seminar with Michel Foucault*, ed. Luther H. Martin, Huck Gutman and Patrick H. Hutton. London: Tavistock.

1988k [1982]. 'The Political Technology of Individuals'. In *Technologies of the Self: A Seminar with Michel Foucault*, ed. Luther H. Martin, Huck Gutman and Patrick H. Hutton. London: Tavistock.

1988l [1983]. 'The Minimalist Self'. In *Politics, Philosophy, Culture: Interviews and Other Writings, 1977–1984*, trans. Alan Sheridan and others, and ed. Lawrence D. Kritzman. New York: Routledge.

1988m [1983]. 'Social Security'. In *Politics, Philosophy, Culture: Interviews and Other Writings, 1977–1984*, trans. Alan Sheridan and others, and ed. Lawrence D. Kritzman. New York: Routledge.

1988n [1983]. 'Contemporary Music and the Public'. In *Politics, Philosophy, Culture: Interviews and Other Writings, 1977–1984*, trans. Alan Sheridan et al., ed. Lawrence D. Kritzman. New York: Routledge.

1988o [1984]. *The Care of the Self: The History of Sexuality, Volume 3*. Trans. Robert Hurley. New York: Vintage.

1988p [1984]. 'The Ethic of Care for the Self as a Practice of Freedom'. Trans. J.D. Gauthier. In *The Final Foucault*, ed. James Bernauer and David Rasmussen. Cambridge, MA: MIT Press.

1988q [1984]. 'An Aesthetics of Existence'. In *Politics, Philosophy, Culture: Interviews and Other Writings, 1977–1984*, trans. Alan Sheridan et al., ed. Lawrence D. Kritzman. New York: Routledge.

1988r [1984]. 'The Return of Morality'. In *Politics, Philosophy, Culture: Interviews and Other Writings, 1977–1984*, trans. Alan Sheridan et al., ed. Lawrence D. Kritzman. New York: Routledge.

1988s [1984]. 'The Concern for Truth'. In *Politics, Philosophy, Culture: Interviews and Other Writings, 1977–1984*, trans. Alan Sheridan et al., ed. Lawrence D. Kritzman. New York: Routledge.

1988t [1966]. 'Behind the Fable'. Trans. Pierre A. Walker. *Critical Texts* 5: 1–5.

1988u [1984]. '(Auto)biography: Michel Foucault 1926–1984'. Trans. Jackie Urla. *History of the Present* (Spring): 13–15.

1989a. *Resumé des Cours, 1970–1982*. Paris: Julliard.

1989b [1981]. *Remarks on Marx: Conversations with Duccio Trombadori*. Trans. R. James Goldstein and James Cascaito. New York: Semiotext(e).

1989c [1975]. 'Photogenic Painting'. Trans. Pierre A. Walker. *Critical Texts* 6(3): 1–12.

1989d [1975]. 'Friendship as a Way of Life'. In *Foucault Live*, trans. John Johnston, ed. Sylvere Lotringer. New York: Semiotext(e).

1990a [1966]. 'Maurice Blanchot: The Thought from Outside'. Trans. Jeffrey Mehlman and Brian Massumi. In *Foucault–Blanchot*. New York: Zone Books.

1990b [1978]. 'Qu'est-ce que la Critique?' Roundtable. *Bulletin de la Société française de la Philosophie* 84(2) (April–June): 35–63.

1991 [1976]. 'Faire Vivre et Laisser Mourir: La Naissance du Racisme'. *Les Temps Modernes* 46(535) (February): 37–61.

1993 [1980]. 'About the Beginning of the Hermeneutics of the Self: Two Lectures at Dartmouth'. *Political Theory* 21(2) (May): 200–27.

Secondary Sources

Alcoff, Linda. 1990. 'Feminist Politics and Foucault: The Limits to a Collaboration'. In *Crises in Continental Philosophy*, ed. Arleen B. Dallery and Charles E. Scott. Albany: SUNY Press.

Ansell-Pearson, Keith. 1991. 'The Significance of Michel Foucault's Reading of Nietzsche: Power, the Subject, and Political Theory'. *Nietzsche-Studien* 20: 267–83.

Bahro, Rudolf. 1978. *The Alternative in Eastern Europe*. Trans. David Fernbach. London: NLB.

Balbus, Isaac D. 1986. 'Disciplining Women: Michel Foucault and the Power of Feminist Discourse'. *Praxis International* 5(4) (January): 466–83.

Bartky, Sandra Lee. 1988. 'Foucault, Femininity, and the Modernization of Patriarchal Power'. In *Feminism and Foucault*, ed. Irene Diamond and Lee Quinby. Boston: Northeastern University Press.

Baudelaire, Charles. 1964. 'The Painter of Modern Life'. In *The Painter of Modern Life and Other Essays*. Trans. and ed. Jonathan Mayne. London: Phaidon.

Baudrillard, Jean. 1980. 'Forgetting Foucault'. Trans. Nicole Dufresne. *Humanities in Society* 3(1) (Winter): 87–111.

Bauman, Zygmunt. 1992. *Intimations of Postmodernity*. London: Routledge.

Bernauer, James. 1990. *Michel Foucault's Force of Flight: Toward an Ethic for Thought*. New Jersey: Humanities Press.

Bernstein, Richard. 1972. *Praxis and Action*. London: Duckworth.

Bersani, Leo. 1988. 'Is the Rectum a Grave?' In *AIDS: Cultural Analysis, Cultural Activism*, ed. Douglas Crimp. Cambridge, MA: MIT Press.

Bird, J.F. 1989. 'Foucault: Power and Politics'. In *Politics and Social Theory*, ed. Peter Lassman. London: Routledge.

Bordo, Susan. 1988. 'Anorexia Nervosa: Psychopathology as the Crystallization of Culture'. In *Feminism and Foucault*, ed. Irene Diamond and Lee Quinby. Boston: Northeastern University Press.

Burchell, Graham. 1991. 'Peculiar Interests: Civil Society and Governing "The System of Natural Liberty"'. In *The Foucault Effect: Studies in Governmentality*, ed. Graham Burchell, Colin Gordon and Peter Miller. Hemel Hempstead: Harvester Wheatsheaf.

Burckhardt, Jacob. 1935. *The Civilization of the Renaissance in Italy*. Trans. S.G.C. Middlemore. USA: Albert and Charles Boni.

Butler, Judith. 1989. 'Foucault and the Paradox of Bodily Inscriptions'. *Journal of Philosophy* 86(11) (November): 601–7.

—— 1990. *Gender Trouble: Feminism and the Subversion of Identity*. New York: Routledge.

Carroll, David. 1987. *Paraesthetics: Foucault, Lyotard, Derrida*. New York: Methuen.

Cocks, Joan. 1989. *The Oppositional Imagination: Feminism, Critique and Political Theory*. London: Routledge.

Cohen, Ed. 1988. 'Foucauldian Necrologies: "Gay Politics"? Politically Gay?'. *Textual Practice* 2(1) (Spring): 87–101.

—— 1991. 'Who Are "We"? Gay Identity as Political (E)motion'. In *Inside/Out*, ed. Diana Fuss. New York: Routledge.

Connolly, William. 1985. 'Taylor, Foucault and Otherness'. *Political Theory* 13(3) (August): 365–76.

—— 1991a. *Identity/Difference: Democratic Negotiations of Political Paradox*. Ithaca: Cornell University Press.

—— 1991b. 'Democracy and Territoriality'. *Millennium* 20(3): 463–84.

—— 1993a. *The Augustinian Imperative: A Reflection on the Politics of Morality*. Newbury Park: Sage.

—— 1993b. 'Beyond Good and Evil: The Ethical Sensibility of Michel Foucault'. *Political Theory* 21(3) (August): 365–89.

d'Amico, Robert. 1989. *Historicism and Knowledge*. New York: Routledge.

Dallmayr, Fred. 1984. 'Pluralism Old and New: Foucault on Power'. In *Polis and Praxis*, ed. Fred Dallmayr. Cambridge, MA: MIT Press.

Davidson, Arnold. 1990. 'Sex and the Emergence of Sexuality'. In *Forms of Desire: Sexual Orientation and the Social Constructionist Controversy*. New York: Garland.

de Lauretis, Teresa. 1987. *Technologies of Gender*. Bloomington: Indiana University Press.

Deleuze, Gilles. 1988. *Foucault*. Trans. Sean Hand. London: Athlone Press.

Dews, Peter. 1987. *Logics of Disintegration: Post-Structuralist Thought and the Claims of Critical Theory*. London: Verso.

—— 1989. 'The Return of the Subject in Late Foucault'. *Radical Philosophy* 51 (Spring): 37–41.

Diamond, Irene and Lee Quinby. 1988. 'American Feminism and the Language of Control'. In *Feminism and Foucault*, ed. Irene Diamond and Lee Quinby. Boston: Northeastern University Press.

Dreyfus, Hubert L. and Paul Rabinow. 1982. *Michel Foucault: Beyond Structuralism and Hermeneutics*. Brighton: Harvester.

Eagleton, Terry. 1990. *The Ideology of the Aesthetic*. Oxford: Basil Blackwell.

Eribon, Didier. 1989. *Michel Foucault*. Paris: Flammarion.

—— 1991. *Michel Foucault*. Trans. Betsy Wing. Cambridge, MA: Harvard University Press.

Flynn, Thomas. 1988. 'Foucault as Parrhesiast: His Last Course at the College de France'. In *The Final Foucault*, ed. James Bernauer and David Rasmussen. Cambridge, MA: MIT Press.

Frankl, Victor. 1962. *Man's Search for Meaning: An Introduction to Logotherapy*. Boston: Beacon Press.

Fraser, Nancy. 1981. 'Foucault on Modern Power: Empirical Insights and Normative Confusions'. *Praxis International* 1(3): 272–87.

—— 1985. 'Michel Foucault: A "Young Conservative"?' *Ethics* 96 (October): 165–84.

Fukuyama, F. 1989. 'The End of History'. *The National Interest* 16 (Summer): 3–18.

Gane, Mike. 1986. 'The Form of Foucault'. *Economy and Society* 15(1) (February): 110–22.

Gillan, Garth. 1988. 'Foucault's Philosophy'. In *The Final Foucault*, ed. James Bernauer and David Rasmussen. Cambridge, MA: MIT Press: 34–44.

Gordon, Colin. 1980. Afterword to *Power/Knowledge: Selected Interviews and Other Writings, 1972–1977*, by Colin Gordon. Brighton: Harvester.

—— 1986. 'Question, Ethos, Event: Foucault on Kant and Enlightenment'. *Economy and Society* 15(1) (February): 71–87.

—— 1987. 'The Soul of the Citizen: Max Weber and Michel Foucault on Rationality and Government'. In *Max Weber, Rationality and Modernity*, ed. Scott Lash and Sam Whimster. London: Allen & Unwin.

—— 1991. 'Governmental Rationality: An Introduction'. In *The Foucault Effect: Studies in Governmentality*, ed. Graham Burchell, Colin Gordon and Peter Miller. London: Harvester Wheatsheaf.

Greenblatt, Stephen. 1980. *Renaissance Self-Fashioning: From More to Shakespeare*. Chicago: University of Chicago Press.

Gutting, Gary. 1989. *Michel Foucault's Archaeology of Scientific Reason*. Cambridge: Cambridge University Press.

Habermas, Jürgen. 1979. 'Legitimation Problems in the Modern State'. In *Communication and the Evolution of Society*, trans. Thomas McCarthy. Boston: Beacon Press.

—— 1983. 'Modernity – An Incomplete Project'. In *Postmodern Culture*, ed. Hal Foster. London: Pluto Press.

—— 1984. *The Theory of Communicative Action*. Vol. 1, *Reason and the Rationalization of Society*. Trans. Thomas McCarthy. Boston: Beacon Press.

—— 1987. *The Philosophical Discourse of Modernity*. Trans. Frederick Lawrence. Cambridge: Polity Press.

Hacking, Ian. 1986. 'The Archaeology of Foucault'. In *Foucault: A Critical Reader*, ed. David Couzens Hoy. Oxford: Basil Blackwell.

Hartsock, Nancy. 1990. 'Foucault on Power: A Theory for Women?' In *Feminism/Postmodernism*, ed. Linda J. Nicholson. New York and London: Routledge.

Hendley, Steven. 1988. 'Power, Knowledge, and Praxis: A Sartrean Approach to a Foucaultian Problem'. *Man and World* 21: 171–89.

Herzog, Don. 1985. *Without Foundations: Justifications in Political Theory*. Ithaca: Cornell University Press.

Hiley, David. 1984. 'Foucault and the Analysis of Power: Political Engagement Without Liberal Hope or Comfort'. *Praxis International* 4 (July): 192–207.

—— 1985. 'Foucault and the Question of Enlightenment'. *Philosophy and Social Criticism* 11 (Summer): 63–84.

Honig, Bonnie. 1993. *Political Theory and the Displacement of Politics*. Ithaca: Cornell University Press.

Hooke, Alexander. 1987. 'The Order of Others: Is Foucault's Antihumanism Against Human Action?' *Political Theory* 15(1) (February): 38–60.

Horowitz, Gad. 1987. 'The Foucaultian Impasse: No Sex, No Self, No Revolution'. *Political Theory* 15(1) (February): 61–80.

Hoy, David Couzens. 1986a. 'Introduction'. In *Foucault: A Critical Reader*, ed. David Couzens Hoy. Oxford: Basil Blackwell.

—— 1986b. 'Power, Repression, Progress: Foucault, Lukes and the Frankfurt School'. In *Foucault: A Critical Reader*, ed. David Couzens Hoy. Oxford: Basil Blackwell.

Ingram, David. 1986. 'Foucault and the Frankfurt School: A Discourse on Nietzsche, Power and Knowledge'. *Praxis International* 6 (October): 311–27.

Kant, Immanuel. 1959. 'What is Enlightenment?' In *Foundations of the Metaphysics of Morals and What is Enlightenment?*, trans. Lewis White Beck. Indianapolis: Bobbs Merrill.

—— 1965. *Critique of Pure Reason*. Trans. Norman Kemp Smith. New York: St Martin's Press.

Keenan, Tom. 1987. 'The "Paradox" of Knowledge and Power: Reading Foucault on a Bias'. *Political Theory* 15(1) (February): 5–37.

Kritzman, Lawrence D. 1988. 'Introduction'. In *Politics, Philosophy, Culture: Interviews and Other Writings, 1977–1984*, ed. Lawrence D. Kritzman. New York: Routledge.

Kundera, Milan. 1984. *The Unbearable Lightness of Being*. London: Faber & Faber.

Lemert, Charles C. and Garth Gillan. 1982. *Michel Foucault: Social Theory and Transgression*. New York: Columbia University Press.

Linden, Robin Ruth, Darlene R. Pagano, Diane E.H. Russel and Susan Leigh Star, eds. 1982. *Against Sadomasochism: A Radical Feminist Analysis*. East Palo Alto: Frog in the Well.

McNay, Lois. 1992. *Foucault and Feminism*. Boston: Northeastern University Press.

Major-Poetzl, Pamela. 1983. *Michel Foucault's Archaeology of Western Culture: Toward a New Science of History*. Chapel Hill: University of North Carolina Press.

Martin, Biddy. 1988. 'Feminism, Criticism, and Foucault'. In *Feminism and Foucault*, ed. Irene Diamond and Lee Quinby. Boston: Northeastern University Press.

Megill, Alan. 1985. *Prophets of Extremity*. Berkeley: University of California Press.

Meisel, Perry. 1979. 'What Foucault Knows'. *Salmagundi* (44–5)(Spring–Summer): 235–41.

Mill, John Stuart. 1975. 'On Liberty'. In *Three Essays: On Liberty; Representative Government; The Subjection of Women*. Oxford: Oxford University Press.

Miller, Peter and Nikolas Rose. 1992. 'Political Power Beyond the State: Problematics of Government'. *British Journal of Sociology* 43 (2): 173–205.

Miller, Peter. 1987. *Domination and Power*. London: Routledge & Kegan Paul.

Miller, James. 1993. *The Passion of Michel Foucault*. New York: Simon & Schuster.

Minson, Jeff. 1985. *Genealogies of Morals: Nietzsche, Foucault, Donzelot and the Eccentricity of Morals*. London: Macmillan.

—— 1986. 'Strategies for Socialists? Foucault's Conception of Power'. In *Towards a Critique of Foucault*, ed. Mike Gane. London: Routledge & Kegan Paul.

Moers, Ellen. 1960. *The Dandy: Brummell to Beerbohm*. London: Secker & Warburg.

Moore, Mary Candace. 1987. 'Ethical Discourse and Foucault's Conception of Ethics'. *Human Studies* 10: 81–95.

Nehamas, Alexander. 1985. *Nietzsche: Life as Literature*. Cambridge, MA: Harvard University Press.

Nelson, Alan. 1986. 'Explanation and Justification in Political Philosophy'. *Ethics* 97 (October): 154–76.

Nietzsche, Friedrich. 1954. 'Homer's Contest'. In *The Portable Nietzsche*, trans. and ed. Walter Kaufmann. New York: Viking.

—— 1956. *The Birth of Tragedy and The Genealogy of Morals*. Trans. Francis Golffing. New York: Doubleday Anchor.

—— 1966. *Beyond Good and Evil: Prelude to a Philosophy of the Future*. New York: Vintage.

—— 1968. *The Will to Power*. Trans. Walter Kaufmann and R.J. Hollingdale. New York: Vintage.

—— 1974. *The Gay Science*. Trans. Walter Kaufmann. New York: Vintage.

—— 1983. *Untimely Meditations*. Trans. R.J. Hollingdale. Cambridge: Cambridge University Press.

Norris, Christopher. 1993. *The Truth About Postmodernism*. Oxford: Basil Blackwell.

Paden, Roger. 1986. 'Locating Foucault – Archaeology vs. Structuralism'. *Philosophy and Social Criticism* 11 (Winter): 19–37.

—— 1987. 'Foucault's Anti-Humanism'. *Human Studies* 10: 123–41.

Pasquino, Pasquale. 1986. 'Michel Foucault (1926–84): The Will to Knowledge'. Trans. Chloe Chard. *Economy and Society* 15(1) (February): 97–109.

Paternek, Margaret A. 1987. 'Norms and Normalization: Michel Foucault's Overextended Panoptic Machine'. *Human Studies* 10: 97–121.

Patton, Paul. 1989. 'Taylor and Foucault on Power and Freedom'. *Political Studies* 37: 260–76.

Philp, Mark. 1983. 'Foucault on Power: A Problem in Radical Translation?' *Political Theory* 11(1) (February): 29–52.

Plant, Raymond. 1991. *Modern Political Thought*. Oxford: Basil Blackwell.

Poulantzas, Nicos. 1978. *State, Power, Socialism*. London: New Left Books.

Rajchman, John. 1985. *Michel Foucault: The Freedom of Philosophy*. New York: Columbia University Press.

—— 1991. *Truth and Eros: Foucault, Lacan, and the Question of Ethics*. New York: Routledge.

Reagon, Bernice Johnson. 1984. 'Coalition Politics: Turning the Century'. In *Home Girls: A Black Feminist Anthology*, ed. Barbara Smith. New York: Kitchen Table/Women of Color Press.

Richters, Annemiek. 1988. 'Modernity–Postmodernity Controversies: Habermas and Foucault'. *Theory, Culture and Society* 5: 611–43.

Ripstein, Arthur. 1987. 'Foundationalism in Political Theory'. *Philosophy and Public Affairs* 16(2) (Spring): 115–37.

Rose, Nikolas. 1990. *Governing the Soul: The Shaping of the Private Self*. London: Routledge.

Said, Edward. 1986. 'Foucault and the Imagination of Power'. In *Foucault: A Critical Reader*, ed. David Couzens Hoy. Oxford: Basil Blackwell.

Samois. 1987. *Coming to Power: Writings and Graphics on Lesbian S/M*. 3rd edn. Boston: Alyson Publications.

Sawicki, Jana. 1988. 'Identity Politics and Sexual Freedom: Foucault and Feminism'.

In *Feminism and Foucault*, ed. Irene Diamond and Lee Quinby. Boston: Northeastern University Press.

—— 1991. *Disciplining Foucault: Feminism, Power and the Body*. New York: Routledge.

Schnädelbach, Herbert. 1992. 'The Face in the Sand: Foucault and the Anthropological Slumber'. In *Philosophical Interventions in the Unfinished Project of Enlightenment*, trans. William Rehg, ed. Axel Honneth, Thomas McCarthy, Claus Offe and Albert Wellmer. Cambridge, MA: MIT Press.

Schneck, Stephen Frederick. 1987. 'Michel Foucault on Power/Discourse, Theory and Practice'. *Human Studies* 10: 15–33.

Scott, J.C. 1990. *Domination and the Arts of Resistance*. New Haven: Yale University Press.

Shapiro, Ian. 1990. *Political Criticism*. Berkeley: University of California Press.

Sharp, Gene. 1985. *Making Europe Unconquerable*. Cambridge, MA: Ballinger.

Sheridan, Alan. 1980. *Michel Foucault: The Will to Truth*. London: Tavistock.

Shumway, David. 1992. *Michel Foucault*. Charlottesville: University Press of Virginia.

Smart, Barry. 1988. *Michel Foucault*. London: Routledge.

Spivak, Gayatri Chakravorty. 1988. 'Can the Subaltern Speak?' In *Marxism and the Interpretation of Culture*, ed. Cary Neslon and Lawrence Grossberg. Urbana: University of Illinois Press.

Taylor, Charles. 1984. 'Foucault on Freedom and Truth'. *Political Theory* 12 (2) (May): 152–83.

—— 1985. 'Connolly, Foucault and Truth'. *Political Theory* 13 (3) (August): 377–85.

—— 1989. 'Taylor and Foucault on Power and Freedom: A Reply'. *Political Studies* 37: 277–81.

—— 1991. *The Ethics of Authenticity*. Cambridge, MA: Harvard University Press.

Thiele, Leslie Paul. 1990. 'The Agony of Politics: The Nietzschean Roots of Foucault's Thought'. *American Political Science Review* 84 (3) (September): 907–25.

Thompson, Mark, ed. 1991. *Leatherfolk: Radical Sex, People, Politics, and Practice*. Boston: Alyson Publication.

Tyler, Carole-Anne. 1991. 'Boys Will Be Girls: The Politics of Gay Drag'. In *Inside/out: Lesbian Theories, Gay Theories*, ed. Diana Fuss. New York: Routledge.

Walzer, Michael. 1985. *Exodus and Revolution*. New York: Basic Books.

—— 1987. *Interpretation and Social Criticism*. Cambridge, MA: Harvard University Press.

—— 1989. *The Company of Critics: Social Criticism and Political Commitment in the Twentieth Century*. London: Peter Haben.

Wapner, Paul. 1989. 'What's Left: Marx, Foucault and Contemporary Problems of Social Change'. *Praxis International* 9(1/2)(April and July): 88–111.

Warren, Mark. 1988. *Nietzsche and Political Thought*. Cambridge, MA: MIT Press.

West, David. 1987. 'Power and Formation: New Foundations for a Radical Concept of Power'. *Inquiry* 30: 137–54.

White, Stephen. 1986. 'Foucault's Challenge to Critical Theory'. *American Political Science Review* 80(2): 419–32.

Wickham, Gary. 1986. 'Power and Power Analysis: Beyond Foucault?' In *Towards a Critique of Foucault*, ed. Mike Gane. London: Routledge & Kegan Paul.

Woodhull, Winifred. 1988. 'Sexuality, Power, and the Question of Rape'. In *Feminism and Foucault*, ed. Irene Diamond and Lee Quinby. Boston: Northeastern University Press.

Index

149